CU00688262

CORFU

TRAVEL GUIDE

Corfu Uncovered: Unlocking the Hidden Gem of Greece's Breathtaking Island Paradise

NICHOLAS Z. ANDREW

Copyright ©2023 Nicholas Z. Andrew

All rights reserved.

Unauthorized reproduction, distribution or use of this content is strictly prohibited without the prior knowledge or written permission of the copyright owner.

"THE MOST BREATHTAKING IMAGES WILL BE THE ONES PAINTED BY YOUR OWN EYES."

Anonymous

TABLE OF CONTENTS

CHAPTER THREE **43**

CHAPTER FOUR **71**

CHAPTER FIVE.........................129

CHAPTER SIX.........................145

CHAPTER SEVEN.........................169

CHAPTER EIGHT 185

CHAPTER NINE 201

CHAPTER ONE

WELCOME TO CORFU

This beautiful island, located in the Ionian Sea, is a popular destination for tourists from around the world. From stunning beaches and crystal-clear waters to ancient ruins and charming villages, Corfu has something for everyone. In this travel guide, we'll provide you with all the information you need to plan the perfect trip to Corfu.

Overview And Brief History Of Corfu

Corfu is a stunning island located in the Ionian Sea, off the northwest coast of Greece. It is the second-largest of the Ionian Islands, and its rich history, cultural diversity, and natural beauty make it a popular destination for tourists from all over the world.

The island has a long and fascinating history, having been inhabited by several civilizations over the centuries. The Greeks, Romans, Byzantines, Venetians, and British have all left their mark on

Corfu, contributing to its unique blend of cultural influences.

Corfu's landscape is characterized by its rugged coastline, with stunning beaches and crystal-clear waters. The island is also home to lush vegetation, olive groves, and vineyards, making it an ideal destination for nature lovers.

Corfu's cuisine is a reflection of its diverse cultural influences, with traditional Greek dishes such as moussaka and souvlaki, as well as Italian-inspired pasta dishes and British favorites such as fish and chips. Local wines, made using native grape varieties, are also a highlight of Corfu's culinary offerings.

The island has a lively nightlife scene, with bars and clubs located throughout the island, particularly in areas such as Kavos, Ipsos, and Sidari. Corfu's markets, such as the Old Town Market in Corfu Town, are a great place to find fresh produce, handmade crafts, and local delicacies.

Corfu's history is rich and varied, dating back to ancient times. The island has been inhabited by various civilizations over the centuries, including the Greeks, Romans, Byzantines, Venetians, and British, each leaving their mark on the island's culture and architecture.

During the 8th century BC, Corfu was first colonized by the Greeks, who established several city-states on the island. The city of Corfu Town, then known as Kerkyra, became a significant center of trade and commerce, attracting merchants and travelers from across the Mediterranean.

In the centuries that followed, Corfu was ruled by various empires, including the Romans, who conquered the island in 229 BC, and the Byzantines, who controlled it from the 4th century AD until the 13th century.

In the 13th century, Corfu was conquered by the Venetians, who ruled the island for over four centuries. During this time, the Venetians built several fortresses and defensive structures to protect the island from invaders, including the Old Fortress and the New Fortress in Corfu Town.

In 1797, the French briefly occupied Corfu, but it was soon handed over to the British as part of the Treaty of Campo Formio. The British ruled the island until 1864, during which time they made significant improvements to the island's infrastructure, including building roads and modernizing the port.

After gaining independence from the Ottoman Empire in the 19th century, Greece annexed Corfu in 1864, and it has remained part of Greece ever since. Today, Corfu is a popular tourist destination, known for its beautiful beaches, historic landmarks, and unique blend of Greek, Italian, and British culture.

Overall, Corfu is a must-visit destination for anyone looking to experience Greece's rich history, cultural diversity, and natural beauty.

Culture

Corfu's culture is a unique blend of Greek, Italian, and British influences, reflecting the island's rich and varied history. The island has been inhabited by many different civilizations over the centuries, each leaving their mark on the local culture.

The Greeks were the first to settle on Corfu, and their influence can still be seen in the island's traditional music and dance. Corfu's folk music is characterized by the use of the bouzouki, a stringed instrument similar to a mandolin, and the accordion. The island is also known for its lively folk dances, such as the "Kalamatianos" and the "Sirtaki".

The Venetians ruled Corfu from 1386 to 1797 and left a lasting mark on the island's architecture and cuisine. Venetian-style buildings can be seen throughout Corfu Town, with their characteristic red-tiled roofs and pastel-colored walls. The Venetians also introduced new foods to the island, such as pasta and pizza, which are still popular today.

The British ruled Corfu from 1815 to 1864 and left their mark on the island's education system and political structure. During their rule, the British introduced English-language schools and established a democratic government on the island. The British also contributed to the island's infrastructure, building roads and improving the port facilities.

Today, Corfu's culture is a vibrant mix of these different influences, with traditional Greek music and dance sitting alongside Italian-inspired cuisine and British-style governance. The island's festivals and celebrations also reflect this diverse heritage, with events such as the "Easter in Corfu" festival, which combines Greek Orthodox traditions with Venetian-style processions, attracting visitors from around the world.

Geography And Location

Corfu is a Greek island located in the Ionian Sea, off the northwest coast of Greece. It is the second-largest of the Ionian Islands, with a total land area of 585 square kilometers (226 square miles). The island is situated at the entrance to the Adriatic Sea and is approximately 69 kilometers (43 miles) long and 28 kilometers (17 miles) wide at its widest point.

The island's topography is characterized by mountainous terrain, with Mount Pantokrator being the highest peak at 906 meters (2,972 feet) above sea level. The mountain range runs along the northeastern side of the island and provides a scenic backdrop to the coastline below.

Corfu's coastline is dotted with numerous bays and coves, as well as sandy and pebble beaches. The island's beaches are some of the most beautiful in Greece, with crystal clear waters that are ideal for swimming and water sports.

The island's capital and largest city is Corfu Town, also known as Kerkyra. It is located on the east coast of the island and has a population of around 30,000 people. The town is a UNESCO World Heritage Site and is renowned for its Venetian-style architecture, narrow streets, and lively atmosphere.

Corfu is situated close to the Albanian coast, with the closest point just 2 kilometers (1.2 miles) away. The island is also within easy reach of other popular Ionian Islands, including Zakynthos, Kefalonia, and Lefkada.

The island's location in the Mediterranean has made it a strategic point for trade and commerce throughout history. The island has been inhabited since ancient times, with evidence of settlement dating back to the Paleolithic era. Over the centuries, Corfu has been ruled by various civilizations, including the Greeks, Romans, Byzantines, Venetians, and British, all of whom have left their mark on the island's history and culture.

Weather And Climate

Corfu enjoys a pleasant Mediterranean climate characterized by warm summers and mild winters. The island's climate is influenced by its location in the Ionian Sea, which brings moderate temperatures and refreshing sea breezes.

Corfu experiences four distinct seasons:

Spring (March to May)

Spring in Corfu is mild and pleasant, with temperatures gradually rising throughout the season. Average temperatures range from 15°C (59°F) to 20°C (68°F), making it an excellent time to explore the island's natural beauty and enjoy outdoor activities.

Summer (June to August)

Summer is the peak tourist season in Corfu, characterized by hot and sunny weather. Average temperatures range from 25°C (77°F) to 30°C (86°F), with occasional heatwaves pushing temperatures even higher. The sea temperature reaches a comfortable 25°C (77°F) to 28°C (82°F), perfect for swimming and water sports.

Autumn (September to November)

Autumn in Corfu is mild and pleasant, with gradually decreasing temperatures. Average temperatures range from 20°C (68°F) to 25°C (77°F) in September, cooling down to 15°C (59°F) to 20°C (68°F) in November. It is a great time to visit for those who prefer milder weather and fewer crowds.

Winter (December to February)

Winters in Corfu are mild compared to many other European destinations. Average temperatures range from 10°C (50°F) to 15°C (59°F). While it is the rainy season, rainfall is still relatively low compared to other parts of Greece. The island's greenery flourishes during this time, and it is a peaceful period to explore its cultural attractions.

Rainfall

Corfu receives most of its rainfall during the winter months, with January and February being the wettest. The island experiences an average of 1,000 mm (39 inches) of rainfall annually. Rain showers are usually short-lived, followed by sunny spells.

Sunshine Hours

Corfu enjoys a significant amount of sunshine throughout the year. During the summer months, the island experiences up to 12 hours of sunshine per day, providing ample time for outdoor activities and beach relaxation. Even during the winter, Corfu receives around 4 to 6 hours of sunshine daily.

Wind

Corfu benefits from refreshing sea breezes, particularly during the summer months. The prevailing winds blow from the northwest, providing relief from the heat and creating favorable conditions for water sports like windsurfing and sailing.

By understanding the weather and climate patterns in Corfu, you can plan your visit accordingly and make the most of your time on this beautiful Greek island.

Best Time To Visit

Corfu has a Mediterranean climate, with hot and dry summers and mild winters. The best time to visit Corfu depends on personal preferences and what activities you plan to do on the island.

The peak tourist season in Corfu runs from June to August when the weather is hot and dry, and the sea is warm enough for swimming. The island is crowded during this time, and prices for accommodation and activities can be higher. However, the nightlife and entertainment options are abundant during this period, and the atmosphere is lively and vibrant.

The shoulder season, which runs from April to May and from September to October, can be an excellent time to visit Corfu. The weather during this time is pleasant, and the sea is warm enough for swimming. The island is less crowded, and prices for accommodation and activities are generally lower. It is also an ideal time for outdoor activities such as hiking, cycling, and exploring the island's natural beauty.

Winter in Corfu is mild and rainy, with temperatures ranging between 10°C to 15°C. It is an off-season period, and many businesses, including hotels, restaurants, and shops, may be closed. However, this is an ideal time to explore the island's historical and cultural sites, as well as its traditional villages, without the crowds.

Overall, the best time to visit Corfu depends on what type of experience you are looking for. If you want a lively and vibrant atmosphere, the summer months are the best time to visit. For those who prefer a more peaceful and relaxing vacation, the shoulder season or winter months may be more suitable.

Visa And Entry Requirements For Corfu

Before traveling to Corfu, it's essential to understand the visa and entry requirements to ensure a smooth and hassle-free journey. The specific requirements may vary depending on your nationality and the purpose and duration of your visit. Here is a comprehensive guide to visa and entry requirements for Corfu:

Visa Exemptions

Citizens of the European Union (EU) and the European Economic Area (EEA) countries, as well as Switzerland, do not need a visa to enter Corfu. They can stay in Greece, including Corfu, for an unlimited period using their valid national identification card or passport.

Schengen Area

Greece, including Corfu, is part of the Schengen Area, which allows for visa-free travel between 26 European countries. If you hold a valid Schengen visa, you can enter Corfu without the need for an additional visa.

Non-Schengen Countries

If you are a citizen of a non-Schengen country, you may need to obtain a visa before traveling to Corfu.

Check with the Greek embassy or consulate in your home country for specific visa requirements and procedures. It's advisable to apply for the visa well in advance of your planned trip.

Visa Types

Depending on the purpose of your visit, you may need to apply for a specific type of visa. The most common visa types for travelers to Corfu include:

Tourist Visa: If you are visiting Corfu for tourism purposes, such as sightseeing, relaxation, or visiting friends and family, you will typically need to apply for a tourist visa.

Business Visa: If you are traveling to Corfu for business-related activities, such as meetings, conferences, or negotiations, you may need to apply for a business visa.

Work Visa: If you intend to work in Corfu, you will need to obtain a work visa. This typically requires sponsorship from an employer in Greece.

Student Visa: If you plan to study in Corfu, such as enrolling in a university or attending a language course, you will need to apply for a student visa.

Visa Application Process

To apply for a visa to Corfu, follow these general steps:

- Determine the type of visa you need based on the purpose of your visit.
- Gather the required documents, which may include a completed application form, passport-sized photos, valid passport, travel itinerary, proof of accommodation, proof of sufficient funds, and travel insurance.
- Schedule an appointment at the Greek embassy or consulate in your home country.
- Attend the appointment and submit your visa application along with the required documents.
- Pay the applicable visa fees.
- Wait for the visa processing time, which can vary depending on your nationality and the embassy/consulate's workload.
- Once your visa is approved, collect your passport and visa.

Passport Requirements

Ensure that your passport meets the following requirements:

Validity: Your passport should be valid for at least six months beyond your intended stay in Corfu.

Blank Pages: Your passport should have sufficient blank pages for visa stamps.

Additional Entry Requirements

In addition to a visa, you may need to fulfill other entry requirements, including:

Return Ticket: It is advisable to have a return ticket or proof of onward travel to show immigration authorities that you intend to leave Corfu within the allowed period.

Sufficient Funds: You may be asked to provide proof of sufficient funds to cover your stay in Corfu, including accommodation, meals, transportation, and other expenses.

Travel Insurance: It is recommended to have travel insurance that covers medical emergencies and repatriation.

Customs Regulations

Familiarize yourself with the customs regulations of Greece to ensure a smooth entry into Corfu and to avoid any legal issues. Some important customs regulations include:

Restricted and Prohibited Items: Greece has restrictions on bringing certain items into the country, such as firearms, drugs, counterfeit goods, and protected species of plants and animals. Familiarize yourself with the list of restricted and prohibited items to avoid any legal complications.

Duty-Free Allowances: If you are arriving from outside the EU, there are duty-free allowances for certain goods, including alcohol, tobacco, and personal belongings. Make sure to comply with these allowances to avoid paying additional customs duties.

Currency Regulations: There are no restrictions on the amount of currency you can bring into Greece. However, if you are carrying a large sum of money (over 10,000 euros or equivalent), you are required to declare it at the customs upon arrival.

Visa Extensions

If you are already in Corfu and wish to extend your stay, it may be possible to apply for a visa extension at the local immigration office. However, visa extensions are subject to specific conditions and limitations. It's advisable to consult the local immigration authorities or a legal representative for guidance on the visa extension process.

Traveling to Other Schengen Countries

If you plan to visit other Schengen countries in addition to Corfu, it's important to note that your visa or visa exemption for Greece allows for travel within the entire Schengen Area. However, ensure that your total stay within the Schengen Area does not exceed the maximum allowed duration specified by the visa or visa exemption.

It's crucial to research and understand the specific visa and entry requirements that apply to your nationality and travel circumstances. For the most accurate and up-to-date information, contact the Greek embassy or consulate in your home country or consult with a reputable travel agency specializing in Greek travel.

Remember to allow ample time for visa processing and gather all necessary documents to ensure a smooth entry into Corfu. By adhering to the visa and entry requirements, you can enjoy your time in Corfu without any legal complications and fully immerse yourself in the beauty and culture of the island.

In conclusion before traveling to Corfu, it's essential to understand the visa and entry requirements to ensure a smooth and hassle-free journey. The specific requirements may vary depending on your nationality and the purpose and duration of your visit. Here is a comprehensive guide to visa and entry requirements for Corfu:

Essential Things To Pack On Your Corfu Trip

When packing for a trip to Corfu, it's important to consider the island's climate, activities, and culture. Here are some essential items to pack for your Corfu trip:

Sunscreen: Corfu is a sunny island with hot weather, especially during the summer months. Sunscreen is essential to protect your skin from harmful UV rays that can cause skin damage or sunburn. It is recommended to bring a sunscreen with a high SPF rating, ideally SPF 30 or higher. It is also recommended to bring a waterproof sunscreen if you plan to spend a lot of time in the water.

Swimsuit: With over 200 kilometers of coastline and countless beaches, a swimsuit is essential when visiting Corfu. Whether you are planning to swim, snorkel, or sunbathe, a comfortable swimsuit will allow you to enjoy the crystal clear waters of the island. It is also recommended to bring a cover-up or a beach dress to wear when leaving the beach or visiting beachfront restaurants.

Comfortable Walking Shoes: Corfu's terrain is varied and can be uneven, especially in the countryside and historical sites. A pair of comfortable walking shoes is essential to keep your feet protected and comfortable while exploring the island. It is recommended to bring shoes with good traction, as some paths can be slippery. Flip flops or sandals can also be useful for beach visits or casual outings.

Lightweight Clothing: Corfu's climate is warm and sunny, especially during the summer months. Lightweight and breathable clothing is essential to stay cool and comfortable. Cotton and linen fabrics are ideal as they allow air to circulate and prevent overheating. It is also recommended to bring a hat or a cap to protect your head from the sun.

Camera: Corfu is a picturesque island with stunning landscapes, beaches, and historical sites. A camera or a smartphone with a good camera is essential to capture the beauty of the island. Don't forget to bring extra batteries, a memory card, or a charger.

Medications: If you take any prescription medications, it is essential to bring them with you. It is also recommended to bring over-the-counter medications such as pain relievers, antihistamines, and stomach remedies. You may also consider bringing a first aid kit for minor injuries or illnesses.

Insect Repellent: Mosquitoes and other insects are common in Corfu, especially during the summer months. It is essential to bring insect repellent to prevent bites and avoid discomfort. It is recommended to use a repellent that contains DEET or a natural alternative such as citronella or eucalyptus oil.

Mosquito Net: If you plan to stay in accommodation without air conditioning or windows with screens, a mosquito net can help protect you from mosquito bites during the night.

Adapter: Greece uses a different electrical plug than many other countries, so it is essential to bring an adapter to charge your electronic devices. It is recommended to bring a universal adapter that can be used in multiple countries.

Cash and Credit Cards: Many businesses in Corfu accept credit cards, but it is still a good idea to carry some cash for smaller purchases and tipping. It is also recommended to inform your bank of your travel plans to avoid any issues with your card.

Travel Documents: Essential travel documents for your trip to Corfu include your passport, visa (if required), travel insurance, and any other important documents such as flight tickets or hotel reservations. It is recommended to keep these documents in a safe and secure place, such as a hotel safe.

Reusable Water Bottle: Staying hydrated is essential in Corfu's hot weather, especially when spending time outdoors or engaging in physical activities. Bringing a reusable water bottle will help you stay hydrated while reducing plastic waste.

Travel Lock - To keep your belongings safe and secure while traveling, pack a travel lock for your luggage. This is especially important if you plan on staying in other shared accommodations.

Respectful Clothing: Corfu is a predominantly Orthodox Christian society, and it is essential to dress respectfully when visiting religious sites. It is recommended to wear clothing that covers your shoulders and knees, especially in churches, monasteries, or other religious sites. It is also important to respect local customs and dress modestly in public areas.

By packing these essential items, you'll be well-prepared for your Corfu trip and ready to make the most of your time on this beautiful island.

CHAPTER TWO

GETTING TO AND AROUND CORFU

Corfu is a popular tourist destination, attracting visitors from all over the world with its stunning beaches, rich history, and unique culture. In this chapter, we will explore the different ways of getting to and around Corfu and provide useful information for travelers.

By Air

Corfu International Airport is the main gateway to the island, serving both domestic and international flights. The airport is located about 3 kilometers south of Corfu Town and is easily accessible by car or taxi.

The airport has modern facilities and is equipped with all the necessary amenities to ensure a comfortable and stress-free travel experience. There are several duty-free shops, cafes, and restaurants where travelers can relax and grab a bite to eat before their flight.

Airlines that operate regular flights to Corfu include Aegean Airlines, Ryanair, and EasyJet, among others. Flights arrive from major cities across Europe, such as London, Berlin, Rome, and Moscow. During the peak tourist season (June to August), there are many flights available, making it easy to plan a trip to the island.

For travelers arriving from Athens, there are frequent connecting flights to Corfu International Airport. The flight takes about 1 hour and is a convenient option for those who want to avoid a long journey by ferry or bus.

Once at the airport, visitors have several options for transportation to their accommodations. Taxis are available outside the arrivals terminal, and the fare to Corfu Town is approximately 10-15 euros. Visitors can also rent a car from one of the several car rental companies available at the airport. This is a good option for those who want to explore the island independently and at their own pace.

Overall, traveling to Corfu by air is a convenient and comfortable option, and the island's modern airport facilities and numerous flight options make it easy to plan a trip from anywhere in Europe.

By Sea

Traveling to Corfu by sea is a popular option for visitors who prefer a more leisurely and scenic journey. The island is well-connected by ferry to several Greek ports, as well as ports in Albania and Italy.

From Greece

There are regular ferry services from several Greek ports, including Igoumenitsa and Patras. Igoumenitsa is the main port for ferries to Corfu and is located on the northwest coast of Greece. Ferries from Igoumenitsa run several times a day, and the journey takes around 90 minutes. Visitors can choose from conventional or high-speed ferries, depending on their preference and schedule. The high-speed ferries take around 45 minutes to reach Corfu and are ideal for visitors who are short on time.

Patras is located on the Peloponnese peninsula in southern Greece and is a popular port for visitors traveling from other parts of the country. Ferries from Patras to Corfu run several times a week, and the journey takes around 7 hours. Visitors can choose from overnight or daytime ferries, depending on their preference and schedule.

From Albania

Corfu is located just a short distance from the Albanian coast, and there are regular ferry services from several Albanian ports, including Saranda and Vlore. The ferry journey from Saranda takes around

30 minutes, while the journey from Vlore takes around 4 hours. Visitors can choose from conventional or high-speed ferries, depending on their preference and schedule.

From Italy

Corfu is also connected by ferry to several ports in Italy, including Brindisi, Bari, and Ancona. The journey from Brindisi takes around 8 hours, while the journey from Bari takes around 9 hours. The journey from Ancona takes around 16 hours, and visitors can choose from overnight or daytime ferries, depending on their preference and schedule.

Ferry Tickets

Ferry tickets can be purchased in advance online or at the port on the day of travel. Visitors are advised to book their tickets in advance, especially during the peak season (July-August), to avoid disappointment.

The cost of ferry tickets varies depending on the port of departure, the type of ferry, and the time of year. Visitors can also bring their cars on the ferry, allowing for more flexibility when exploring the island. Car rental services are available at the port in Corfu Town for visitors who choose to bring their cars on the ferry.

By Bus

For visitors traveling from other parts of Greece, there are regular bus services to Corfu from major cities such as Athens and Thessaloniki. The bus journey from Athens takes around 8 hours and can be booked in advance online or at the bus station. The buses are comfortable and air-conditioned, with reclining seats and ample legroom for a comfortable journey.

The KTEL bus service is the primary provider of bus services on the island of Corfu, offering regular services to and from Corfu Town, as well as to other parts of the island. There are also private bus companies that offer services to and from other parts of Greece, such as Athens and Thessaloniki.

For those arriving in Corfu by bus, the bus station is located in the center of Corfu Town, just a short walk from the historic Old Town. From here, visitors can easily access other parts of the island using the KTEL bus service or by renting a car.

It's worth noting that during peak season, the buses can get quite crowded, so it's advisable to book tickets in advance and arrive early to ensure a seat. The bus service can also be affected by strikes and disruptions, particularly during the summer months, so it's worth checking with the bus company before traveling to avoid any inconvenience.

Overall, the bus is a cost-effective and convenient way to travel to Corfu, particularly for visitors on a budget. It's also a great way to see the scenic countryside of Greece and enjoy the journey to the island.

By Car

Driving to Corfu is a great option for those who prefer the flexibility and convenience of having their own vehicle to explore the island. However, visitors should be aware that driving in Greece can be challenging, especially for those who are not used to the local driving laws and regulations.

The island of Corfu can be reached by car via the Egnatia Odos highway from Athens or the A2/E90 highway from Thessaloniki. The journey from Athens takes around 7-8 hours, while the journey from Thessaloniki takes around 10 hours, depending on traffic and road conditions. Visitors should plan their route carefully and make sure to take into account the time required for ferry crossings if coming from the mainland.

Car rental services are available at Corfu International Airport and in Corfu Town, with a wide range of vehicles on offer to suit all budgets and preferences. Visitors should ensure they have a valid driver's license and insurance, as well as a credit card for security purposes.

Driving in Corfu can be an enjoyable and rewarding experience, with many scenic routes and picturesque villages to explore. However, visitors should be aware that the roads can be narrow and winding, with steep inclines and declines in some areas. It is also important to be aware of local driving laws, such as the requirement to wear seatbelts and the speed limits, which can vary depending on the type of road.

Visitors should also be aware that parking can be difficult in some areas of Corfu, especially in the high season when the island is more crowded. It is recommended to park in designated parking areas or use private parking facilities, as parking on the side of the road may result in a fine.

Overall, driving to Corfu can be a great way to explore the island at your own pace and enjoy the scenic beauty of the island. However, visitors should exercise caution and familiarize themselves with local driving laws and regulations to ensure a safe and enjoyable trip.

By Cruise Ship

Corfu is a popular destination for cruise ships, with several companies offering Mediterranean cruises that include a stop in Corfu. Cruise ships dock at the port in Corfu Town, where visitors can explore the historic Old Town or take a tour of the island's scenic countryside.

Cruise Lines

Several major cruise lines offer itineraries that include a stop in Corfu. These cruise lines provide a range of options to suit different budgets and interests, from luxury cruises to family-friendly ships. Some of the most popular cruise lines that visit Corfu include:

Royal Caribbean International: This American-based cruise line offers several Mediterranean itineraries that include a stop in Corfu. Ships in the Royal Caribbean fleet range in size from the intimate Empress of the Seas to the massive Symphony of the Seas, and offer a range of amenities such as rock climbing walls, Broadway-style shows, and water parks.

Princess Cruises: This American-based cruise line offers a number of Mediterranean itineraries that stop in Corfu. Ships in the Princess fleet include the luxurious Royal Princess, which offers a range of amenities such as a spa, fitness center, and live entertainment.

Celebrity Cruises: This American-based cruise line offers a variety of itineraries that include a stop in Corfu. Ships in the Celebrity fleet range in size from the intimate Celebrity Xperience to the luxurious Celebrity Edge, and offer a range of amenities such as specialty restaurants, outdoor movie theaters, and wine tastings.

MSC Cruises: This Italian-based cruise line offers a range of Mediterranean itineraries that stop in Corfu. MSC ships range in size from the elegant MSC Divina to the modern MSC Seaview, and offer a range of amenities such as spas, casinos, and live entertainment.

Norwegian Cruise Line: This American-based cruise line offers several Mediterranean itineraries that stop in Corfu. Ships in the Norwegian fleet include the family-friendly Norwegian Bliss, which features a go-kart track and laser tag, and the luxurious Norwegian Spirit, which offers a range of specialty restaurants and a spa.

Holland America Line: This American-based cruise line offers several Mediterranean itineraries that stop in Corfu. Ships in the Holland America fleet include the classic ms Rotterdam, which features a culinary arts center and a theater, and the modern ms Koningsdam, which offers a range of dining options and a spa.

These cruise lines offer a range of onboard activities and amenities, including live entertainment, specialty restaurants, and spa services. Many also offer shore excursions to popular attractions on the island, such as the Achilleion Palace and Paleokastritsa Beach.

Getting Around Corfu

Corfu is a beautiful island in the Ionian Sea with a rich history, stunning beaches, and picturesque villages. To fully experience all that the island has to offer, it is important to know how to get around. This section will provide you with the information you need to navigate Corfu's transportation options.

By Car

Renting a car is a popular option for travelers who want to explore Corfu independently and at their own pace. There are several rental companies on the island, and rental rates are generally reasonable. There are several car rental companies operating in Corfu, both international and local. Some of the most popular car rental companies in Corfu include Hertz, Europcar, Avis, Budget, and Enterprise.

It is recommended to book your car rental in advance, especially during the peak tourist season (July and August), as availability can be limited. You can book your car rental online through the rental company's website or through a travel booking website.

However, there are some important things to consider before renting a car in Corfu.

Firstly, driving in Corfu can be challenging, especially in the narrow streets of Corfu Town and the winding mountain roads. It is important to be cautious and alert, especially when driving at night or in bad weather conditions. It is also important to note that the minimum driving age in Greece is 21 years old and that a valid international driving permit is required.

When renting a car, be sure to inspect it carefully for any damage before you take it out. Make note of any scratches, dents, or other damage, and take photos if necessary. This will help you avoid being charged for any pre-existing damage when you return the car.

In terms of parking, there are several public parking lots and street parking options available in Corfu Town and other major towns on the island. However, parking can be difficult to find during peak tourist season, and you may need to park further away from your destination and walk.

One of the advantages of renting a car is the freedom to explore Corfu's countryside and hidden beaches. There are several scenic drives on the island, including the road from Corfu Town to Paleokastritsa, which offers stunning views of the coastline and the surrounding hills. Another popular drive is the road from Benitses to Lefkimmi, which takes you through traditional villages and past olive groves.

It is also important to note that gas stations can be scarce outside of major towns on the island, so be sure to fill up your tank before setting out on a long drive.

When choosing a rental car, consider the size and type of vehicle that will suit your needs. If you plan to explore Corfu's countryside and visit remote villages, a four-wheel drive or SUV may be more suitable than a compact car. On the other hand, if you are only planning to explore Corfu Town and other urban areas, a smaller car may be more convenient.

Overall, renting a car can be a great way to explore Corfu's natural beauty and historical sites, but it is important to be cautious and responsible while driving.

By Scooter or ATV

Scooters and ATVs are a popular mode of transportation on the island, especially among younger travelers. They offer a fun and convenient way to explore the island's many beaches, villages, and attractions. Rental rates for scooters and ATVs are relatively low, with prices varying depending on the type of vehicle and the rental period. Many rental companies offer discounts for longer rental periods, so it is worth considering renting for several days or even a week.

One of the benefits of renting a scooter or ATV is that they are small and easy to maneuver, allowing you to explore even the narrowest streets and alleys. This is particularly helpful in the historic center of Corfu Town, where many of the streets are too narrow for cars. Additionally, scooters and ATVs are ideal for exploring the island's mountainous terrain, where roads can be steep and winding. They also allow you to reach secluded beaches and coves that may be difficult to access by car.

However, it is important to wear a helmet and to be cautious when driving a scooter or ATV, as accidents can occur. It is also important to note that the minimum driving age for scooters and ATVs in Greece is 18 years old and a valid international driving permit is required. Some rental companies may also require a deposit, which will be returned at the end of the rental period if the vehicle is returned undamaged.

When renting a scooter or ATV, it is important to inspect the vehicle before renting and to document any existing damage. This will ensure that you are not held responsible for any damage that may have occurred before you rented the vehicle. It is also important to make sure that the rental company provides insurance coverage, as this will protect you in case of an accident.

Overall, renting a scooter or ATV is a popular and convenient way to explore Corfu. They are small and easy to maneuver, allowing you to explore even the narrowest streets and alleys. However, it is important to wear a helmet, be cautious when driving, and to make sure that you have the required documentation and insurance coverage.

By Bicycle

Cycling is a popular way to get around Corfu, and it's an eco-friendly and affordable way to explore the island. There are several bike rental companies on the island, and many hotels also offer bike rentals. Rental rates are relatively cheap, and you can choose from a variety of bikes, including mountain bikes, road bikes, and e-bikes.

Corfu has a network of cycling paths that are well-maintained and offer scenic views of the island's countryside. One of the most popular cycling routes is the Corfu Trail, which is a 220 km long-distance footpath that runs from the south to the north of the island. The Corfu Trail is also suitable for cycling, and it offers a unique way to explore the island's natural beauty.

However, it's important to note that some of the roads in Corfu can be steep and challenging for inexperienced cyclists. It's recommended that you wear a helmet and bring plenty of water and snacks, especially if you're planning on cycling in the summer when temperatures can get hot. You should also be aware of the traffic and follow the rules of the road.

If you're not confident cycling alone, you can join a guided cycling tour. There are several tour operators on the island that offer guided cycling tours, ranging from half-day tours to multi-day tours. These tours are led by experienced guides who know the best routes and can show you the hidden gems of the island.

Some popular cycling routes on the island include the Achilleion Palace route, which takes you through the picturesque villages of Gastouri and Agios Ioannis and offers stunning views of the palace and the surrounding countryside. Another popular route is the Old Perithia route, which takes you through the abandoned village of Old Perithia and offers a glimpse into the island's rich history.

Overall, cycling is a great way to explore Corfu, and it allows you to get up close and personal with the island's natural beauty and cultural heritage. Whether you're an experienced cyclist or a casual rider, there's something for everyone on the island's cycling trails.

By Bus

Corfu has a well-developed public bus network that connects all major towns and villages on the island. The buses are operated by KTEL, which is the main public transportation company in Greece. The buses are relatively cheap and offer a convenient way to travel around the island.

There are two main bus stations in Corfu, one in Corfu Town and the other in San Rocco Square, located in the new port area. The schedules and routes are posted at the bus stations, and you can also find them online or in local travel agencies. The bus schedules can be subject to change, especially during peak tourist season, so it's important to confirm the schedules beforehand.

The buses in Corfu are typically comfortable and air-conditioned, which is especially important during the hot summer months. Most of the buses have several stops along the way, so you can get off at any destination you want. The bus drivers are usually friendly and helpful, so if you're unsure of where to get off, don't hesitate to ask for assistance.

The bus fares in Corfu are relatively low, with a one-way ticket typically costing between 1.50-2.50 euros, depending on the distance. You can purchase the tickets on the bus, but it's important to have exact change as the drivers may not always have change available. You can also purchase a "KTEL Card," which is a reloadable smart card that offers discounts on bus fares.

One thing to keep in mind when taking the bus in Corfu is that it can be crowded, especially during peak tourist season. If you're traveling with a lot of luggage, it may be challenging to find space on the bus. Additionally, the buses can be subject to delays due to traffic congestion or other factors, so it's important to plan accordingly.

Overall, taking the bus in Corfu is a convenient and affordable way to get around the island. It's also a great way to meet locals and other travelers and get a glimpse into daily life on the island.

By Taxi

Taxis are a convenient and comfortable way to get around Corfu, especially if you are traveling in a group or have a lot of luggage. Taxis are easily available at the airport, ferry ports, and in Corfu Town. It is also possible to hail a taxi on the street or call for one using a taxi app.

In Corfu, taxis are usually white with a distinctive green stripe on the side, and they have a taxi sign on the roof. The fare is calculated based on the distance traveled and the time of day. Taxis charge a higher rate at night and on Sundays and public holidays.

It is important to agree on the fare before getting into the taxi, as some taxi drivers may try to charge more than the standard fare. The standard fare from the airport to Corfu Town is around €15-20, while a taxi ride from Corfu Town to the popular resort of Paleokastritsa can cost around €35-40.

If you are traveling to a remote area or a small village, it is important to make sure the taxi driver knows the exact location, as some drivers may not be familiar with all areas of the island. It is also important to carry cash, as many taxi drivers do not accept credit cards.

Finally, it is worth noting that some taxi drivers may offer guided tours of the island, which can be a great way to explore Corfu's hidden gems. However, be sure to negotiate the price in advance and to make sure the taxi driver has a valid license before embarking on a guided tour.

You should note that the prices of fares may be effected by time of the day, amount of luggage and type of vehicle

Overall, taxis are a comfortable and convenient way to get around Corfu, especially for short trips or if you are traveling in a group. Just be sure to agree on the fare in advance and to carry cash, as credit cards may not be accepted. With a little planning, a taxi ride can be a stress-free way to explore the island's beautiful scenery and vibrant culture.

By Boat

Corfu's beautiful coastline and clear blue waters make it an ideal destination for exploring by boat. There are several tour operators on the island that offer day trips to nearby islands and secluded coves, and there are also regular ferry services to destinations such as Paxos and Antipaxos. Private boat rentals are also available, allowing you to explore the island's hidden beaches and coves at your own pace.

One of the most popular boat trips is to the nearby island of Paxos, which is known for its crystal-clear waters and secluded beaches. The ferry ride from Corfu to Paxos takes approximately one hour, and there are several ferry services available throughout the day. Once on the island, you can rent a boat or take a guided tour to explore the island's stunning coastline.

Another popular boat trip is to the nearby island of Antipaxos, which is known for its white sand beaches and turquoise waters. The ferry ride from

Corfu to Antipaxos takes approximately one hour and is available from the port of Gaios on Paxos. Once on the island, you can relax on the beaches or go snorkeling in the crystal-clear waters.

Private boat rentals are also available on Corfu, allowing you to explore the island's hidden coves and beaches at your own pace. Boat rentals are available for full or half-day rentals, and prices vary depending on the type of boat and the length of the rental. With a private boat rental, you can explore the island's coastline, visit secluded coves and beaches, and even go fishing.

It is important to note that boat trips and rentals are weather-dependent, and it is always a good idea to check the weather forecast before booking a boat trip or rental. It is also important to follow all safety guidelines and to wear life jackets at all times while on the water.

Overall, exploring Corfu by boat is a must-do activity for any traveler to the island. Whether you opt for a guided tour, a ferry ride, or a private boat rental, you are sure to be amazed by the island's stunning coastline and clear blue waters.

In conclusion, there are several transportation options available for getting around Corfu, including rental cars, scooters, bicycles, buses, taxis, and boats. Each mode of transportation has its own advantages and disadvantages, and the choice will depend on your budget, travel style, and personal preferences. Regardless of how you choose to get around, be sure to take the time to explore the island's beautiful scenery, historical sites, and vibrant culture.

CHAPTER THREE

ACCOMMODATION IN CORFU

Corfu offers a variety of accommodation options to suit every budget and preference, from luxury resorts to budget-friendly hotels, villas, and apartments.

Hotels

Corfu's hotels offer visitors a variety of options, from luxurious five-star resorts to more affordable three-star properties. Here are some additional details about the different types of hotels available on the island:

Luxury Hotels

Luxury hotels in Corfu offer the ultimate in comfort, relaxation, and indulgence. Here are some additional details about the different types of luxury hotels available on the island:

Five-star resorts

Corfu has several five-star resorts that offer guests the highest level of luxury and service. These resorts often feature extensive grounds with beautiful gardens, private beaches, multiple swimming pools, and a range of dining options.

The Ikos Dassia is one of the most popular five-star resorts on the island. This all-inclusive resort features over 400 rooms and suites, private beach access, seven swimming pools, and a range of activities and excursions included in the room rate. Guests can dine at a variety of on-site restaurants, including one with a Michelin-starred menu.

Other popular five-star resorts in Corfu include the MarBella Corfu Hotel, which offers stunning sea views and a range of on-site activities such as tennis and water sports, and the Domes Miramare, which is located in a historic building and offers a range of luxurious rooms and suites with private pools and sea views.

Boutique hotels

For those seeking a more intimate and personalized luxury experience, Corfu has several boutique hotels that offer a unique blend of traditional charm and modern amenities. These hotels often feature historic buildings, beautiful gardens, and unique décor, and offer guests a more individualized level of service.

The Mayor Mon Repos Palace Art Hotel is a popular boutique hotel in Corfu Town, housed in a historic building that was once a royal residence. The hotel features a range of luxurious rooms and suites, a restaurant with panoramic sea views, and a spa offering a range of treatments.

Other popular boutique hotels in Corfu include the Corfu Mare Boutique Hotel, which offers stylish and comfortable rooms and suites with private balconies, and the Bella Venezia Hotel, which is located in a historic building in the heart of Corfu Town and features elegant rooms and a rooftop terrace with stunning views of the city.

Villas and private residences

For those seeking the ultimate in privacy and luxury, Corfu has several villas and private residences available for rent. These properties often feature extensive grounds with private pools, beautiful gardens, and stunning sea views, and offer guests a completely customized experience with personalized service and amenities.

The Villa Oliva is one of the most popular luxury villas in Corfu, offering guests a beautiful private residence with panoramic sea views, a private pool, and access to a secluded beach. The villa features five bedrooms, a fully equipped kitchen, and a range of indoor and outdoor living spaces for relaxing and entertaining.

Other popular luxury villas in Corfu include the Villa Piedra, which is located in the tranquil village of Agios Stefanos and offers a range of luxurious amenities including a private pool and a home cinema, and the Villa Viola, which is located on the west coast of the island and offers stunning sea views and a range of luxurious amenities such as a private chef and a personal concierge.

Mid-range hotels

Mid-range hotels in Corfu offer a comfortable and affordable accommodation option for visitors who are looking for a balance between luxury and budget. These hotels offer a range of amenities and services, including on-site restaurants, swimming pools, and fitness facilities. Here are some more details about mid-range hotels in Corfu:

Ariti Grand Hotel

Located in Corfu Town, the Ariti Grand Hotel is a popular mid-range hotel that offers comfortable rooms and a range of facilities. The hotel has 156 rooms and suites, all of which are air-conditioned and feature a private balcony or terrace. Room amenities include a mini-fridge, flat-screen TV, and tea and coffee making facilities.

The hotel's outdoor pool is surrounded by a sun terrace with loungers and parasols, and there is also a pool bar serving drinks and snacks throughout the day. The hotel's rooftop terrace offers stunning views of the city and the sea, and is a great spot for a drink or a meal at the hotel's rooftop restaurant.

Other facilities at the Ariti Grand Hotel include a fitness center, a sauna, and a steam room. The hotel also offers a range of services, including 24-hour reception, luggage storage, and car rental.

Bella Venezia Hotel

The Bella Venezia Hotel is located in the heart of Corfu Town, just a few minutes' walk from the city's main attractions. The hotel is housed in a restored 19th-century mansion and offers a range of comfortable rooms and suites.

All rooms at the Bella Venezia Hotel are air-conditioned and feature a flat-screen TV, a mini-bar, and tea and coffee making facilities. Some rooms also have a private balcony or terrace with views of the city.

The hotel's on-site restaurant serves a range of Mediterranean and international cuisine, and there is also a bar and lounge area for drinks and snacks. Other facilities at the hotel include a fitness center, a sauna, and a Jacuzzi.

Divani Corfu Palace

Located in the Kanoni area of Corfu, the Divani Corfu Palace is a mid-range hotel that offers comfortable rooms and a range of facilities. The hotel has 162 rooms and suites, all of which are air-conditioned and feature a private balcony or terrace.

The hotel's outdoor pool is surrounded by a sun terrace with loungers and parasols, and there is also a pool bar serving drinks and snacks throughout the day. The hotel's on-site restaurant serves a range of Greek and international cuisine, and there is also a bar and lounge area for drinks and snacks.

Other facilities at the Divani Corfu Palace include a fitness center, a sauna, and a tennis court. The hotel also offers a range of services, including 24-hour reception, room service, and car rental.

In summary, mid-range hotels in Corfu offer a range of comfortable rooms and facilities at a more affordable price point than luxury hotels. Whether you're staying in Corfu Town or in a quieter area of the island, there are plenty of mid-range hotel options to choose from.

Budget Hotels

Budget hotels are a great option for travelers who want to keep their expenses low while still enjoying the beauty and charm of Corfu. These hotels may not offer the same level of luxury and amenities as higher-end options, but they provide clean and comfortable accommodations at an affordable price. Here are some additional details about budget hotels in Corfu:

Hotel Bretagne

The Hotel Bretagne is a popular budget option located in the heart of Corfu Town. The hotel has several guest rooms, ranging from singles to triples, all of which feature basic amenities such as air conditioning, free Wi-Fi, and a private bathroom. The hotel also has a small garden and terrace, as well as a cozy bar and lounge area.

Despite its budget-friendly prices, the Hotel Bretagne receives consistently high reviews for its cleanliness, friendly staff, and convenient location. Guests can easily explore the historic town center on foot, as well as visit nearby attractions such as the Old Fortress and the Liston promenade.

Hermes Hotel

The Hermes Hotel is another budget option located in Corfu Town, just a short walk from the historic center. The hotel has several guest rooms, each of which features air conditioning, free Wi-Fi, and a private balcony or terrace. The hotel also has a swimming pool, a restaurant serving Greek and international cuisine, and a bar.

While the Hermes Hotel is not as centrally located as some other budget hotels in Corfu Town, guests can easily reach the town center on foot or by public transportation. The hotel's friendly staff and affordable prices make it a popular choice for budget-conscious travelers.

Hotel Roulis

Located in the village of Benitses on the east coast of the island, the Hotel Roulis is a budget-friendly option that offers easy access to the beach and a range of local restaurants and shops. The hotel has several guest rooms, each of which features air conditioning, free Wi-Fi, and a private balcony or terrace with sea or mountain views.

The Hotel Roulis also has a swimming pool, a bar, and a restaurant serving traditional Greek dishes. While the hotel is not as centrally located as some other options on the island, it offers a quieter, more relaxed atmosphere and is a great option for travelers who want to explore the eastern side of Corfu.

Overall, budget hotels in Corfu offer travelers a simple and affordable option for their stay on the island. While they may not offer the same level of luxury and amenities as higher-end hotels, they provide clean and comfortable accommodations at a great value.

Villas And Apartments

Villas and apartments in Corfu offer visitors a more independent and private accommodation option compared to hotels. They are ideal for families or groups of friends who want more space and flexibility during their stay on the island. Villas and apartments are available in a variety of sizes, styles, and locations, ranging from traditional stone houses in quiet villages to modern and minimalist properties with sea views.

One of the advantages of renting a villa or apartment in Corfu is the ability to immerse yourself in the local culture. Many of these properties are located in quieter areas, away from the main tourist hotspots, allowing visitors to experience the island's traditional way of life. Guests can visit local markets, shops, and restaurants, interact with the locals, and discover hidden gems that they might otherwise miss.

Villas and apartments in Corfu are usually fully furnished and equipped with all the amenities needed for a comfortable stay, such as a kitchen, living area, bedrooms, and bathrooms. Some properties also have additional features such as a swimming pool, garden, or terrace, providing guests with a relaxing and peaceful environment to unwind.

Renting a villa or apartment in Corfu is also a cost-effective option for those traveling with a group or family. Instead of paying for multiple hotel rooms, guests can rent a single property, splitting the cost between them. This can make it a more affordable option, especially for longer stays.

One of the most popular areas for villas and apartments in Corfu is the village of Kassiopi, located on the northeast coast of the island. Kassiopi is a charming fishing village that has developed into a popular tourist destination. It is known for its picturesque harbor, ancient ruins, and beautiful beaches. Visitors can rent a villa or apartment in Kassiopi and enjoy its laid-back atmosphere, while still having access to amenities such as restaurants, shops, and bars.

Other popular areas for villas and apartments in Corfu include Agios Stefanos, a quiet village on the northwestern coast of the island, and Paleokastritsa, a scenic area known for its crystal-clear waters and rugged coastline.

In summary, villas and apartments in Corfu offer visitors a more independent and authentic accommodation option, with a range of styles and locations to suit every taste and budget. They provide a comfortable and cost-effective alternative to hotels, allowing guests to experience the island's culture and way of life in a more relaxed and peaceful setting.

Luxury Resorts

Corfu's luxurious resorts offer visitors the ultimate holiday experience with their stunning locations, world-class amenities, and exceptional service. Here are some of the best luxury resorts on the island:

MarBella Corfu Hotel

The MarBella Corfu Hotel is one of the most sought-after luxury resorts in Corfu. Located on the island's east coast, this five-star resort boasts a prime beachfront location and breathtaking views of the Ionian Sea. The resort features a private beach, multiple swimming pools, and a range of water sports activities, including windsurfing, paddleboarding, and kayaking.

Guests can indulge in a variety of spa treatments at the resort's spa, which features a sauna, steam room, and indoor pool. The resort also boasts several restaurants and bars, including the La Bussola Restaurant, which has been awarded a Michelin star. Other dining options include the Platea Greek Restaurant, the Splash Pool Bar, and the Eleonas Beach Bar.

The resort's accommodations range from luxurious rooms to spacious suites and villas, all featuring modern amenities and stunning sea views. Some of the rooms even have private pools, making them perfect for couples seeking a romantic getaway.

Domes Miramare, a Luxury Collection Resort

The Domes Miramare, a Luxury Collection Resort, is a five-star resort located on the island's west coast. This luxurious property was designed by the renowned architect, Gio Ponti, and features an elegant and sophisticated decor. The resort is located in a picturesque setting overlooking the Ionian Sea and features an infinity pool, private beach, and a range of spa treatments.

Guests can enjoy fine dining at the resort's restaurants, including the Michelin-starred restaurant, Il Cortile, which serves Mediterranean cuisine with a modern twist. Other dining options include the Raw Bar, which serves fresh seafood and sushi, and the Beach House, which offers a casual beachfront dining experience.

The resort's accommodations are spacious and stylish, featuring contemporary decor and modern amenities. The rooms and suites offer stunning sea views and some even have private pools or Jacuzzis.

Ikos Dassia

The Ikos Dassia is a luxurious all-inclusive resort located on the island's east coast. This five-star resort offers a range of amenities and activities, including a private beach, multiple swimming pools, and a kids club.

Guests can indulge in a variety of dining options, including six restaurants offering a range of international and local cuisine. The resort also features several bars, including a beach bar, pool bar, and cocktail bar.

The resort's accommodations range from spacious rooms to luxurious suites, all featuring modern amenities and contemporary decor. Some of the rooms and suites offer stunning sea views, while others have private pools or Jacuzzis.

Rodostamo Hotel & Spa
The Rodostamo Hotel & Spa is a luxurious five-star resort located on the island's east coast, just a short distance from Corfu Town. This elegant property is nestled in a lush green landscape and offers stunning views of the Ionian Sea.

Guests can enjoy a range of amenities, including a private beach, infinity pool, and a state-of-the-art spa. The resort also features several restaurants and bars, including the Mura Restaurant, which serves Mediterranean cuisine with a modern twist. Other dining options include the Thalassa Pool Bar, which offers light snacks and cocktails, and the H20 Beach Bar, which serves drinks and snacks on the beach.

The resort's accommodations are spacious and stylish, featuring contemporary decor and modern amenities. The rooms and suites offer stunning sea or garden views, and some even have private pools or Jacuzzis.

Kontokali Bay Resort & Spa

The Kontokali Bay Resort & Spa is a luxurious five-star resort located on the island's central east coast, just a short distance from Corfu Town. The resort is situated in a stunning beachfront location and features lush gardens and panoramic sea views.

Guests can enjoy a range of amenities, including a private beach, multiple swimming pools, and a state-of-the-art spa. The resort also features several restaurants and bars, including the Horizon Restaurant, which serves Mediterranean cuisine with a modern twist. Other dining options include the a la carte restaurant, Yali, and the beach bar, which serves light snacks and cocktails.

The resort's accommodations are spacious and luxurious, featuring contemporary decor and modern amenities. The rooms and suites offer stunning sea or garden views, and some even have private pools or Jacuzzis.

Grecotel Corfu Imperial

The Grecotel Corfu Imperial is a luxurious five-star resort located on the island's east coast, just a short distance from Corfu Town. This elegant property is set in lush gardens and offers stunning views of the Ionian Sea.

Guests can enjoy a range of amenities, including a private beach, multiple swimming pools, and a range of water sports activities. The resort also features several restaurants and bars, including the Aristos Restaurant, which serves Mediterranean cuisine with a modern twist. Other dining options include the Poseidon Pool Bar, which offers light snacks and cocktails, and the Champagne Bar, which serves a variety of wines and champagnes.
The resort's accommodations are spacious and stylish, featuring contemporary decor and modern amenities. The rooms and suites offer stunning sea or garden views, and some even have private pools or Jacuzzis.

Overall, Corfu's luxury resorts offer visitors the ultimate holiday experience with their stunning locations, exceptional amenities, and exceptional service. Whether you're seeking a romantic getaway, a family vacation, or a luxurious escape, these resorts are sure to exceed your expectations.

Overall, Corfu's luxury resorts offer visitors a world-class holiday experience with their stunning locations, exceptional amenities, and exceptional service. Whether you're seeking a romantic getaway, a family vacation, or a luxurious escape, these resorts are sure to exceed your expectations.

Budget-Friendly Accommodation

Corfu is not just a destination for those seeking luxury and opulence, but also for budget-conscious travelers who want to explore the island without breaking the bank. Thankfully, there are several budget-friendly accommodation options in Corfu, including budget hotels, hostels, and guesthouses. These options offer comfortable and affordable accommodations, allowing travelers to spend more money on experiences and activities rather than accommodations.

Budget-friendly accommodations in Corfu can be found throughout the island, including in popular tourist areas like Corfu Town, Gouvia, and Sidari. Here are some of the best budget-friendly accommodation options in Corfu:

Budget Hotels

Corfu has several budget hotels that offer clean and comfortable accommodations at an affordable price. These hotels are typically small, family-run properties located in quieter areas away from the main tourist centers.

One popular budget hotel in Corfu is the Anita Hotel, located in the village of Perama on the east coast of the island. This hotel offers basic but comfortable accommodations, with each room featuring a balcony or terrace and views of the sea or the surrounding countryside. The hotel also has a swimming pool and a restaurant serving traditional Greek cuisine.

Another budget hotel option is the Athina Hotel, located in the village of Gouvia on the east coast of the island. This hotel offers simple but comfortable accommodations, with each room featuring air conditioning and a private balcony or terrace. The hotel also has a swimming pool and a restaurant serving breakfast and dinner.

Hostels

Hostels are a popular accommodation option for budget-conscious travelers, offering affordable rates and a social atmosphere. Corfu has several hostels scattered around the island, each with its own unique vibe and range of facilities.

Pink Palace Hostel
The Pink Palace Hostel is located in the village of Agios Gordios on the west coast of the island and is one of the most popular hostels in Corfu. This hostel offers both dormitory-style and private rooms, with the dorms accommodating up to 10 people. All rooms have shared bathroom facilities.

The Pink Palace Hostel offers a range of facilities and activities, including a swimming pool, beach access, and a nightclub. The hostel also has a restaurant and bar, serving a range of international and local dishes. Guests can participate in a range of activities and tours organized by the hostel, including hiking, kayaking, and quad bike tours.

Corfu Backpackers
The Corfu Backpackers hostel is located in the village of Benitses on the east coast of the island. This hostel offers both dormitory-style and private rooms, with the dorms accommodating up to six people. All rooms have shared bathroom facilities.

The Corfu Backpackers hostel features a communal kitchen and outdoor terrace, as well as a lounge area with a TV and games. The hostel also organizes regular activities and events, including movie nights, BBQs, and pub crawls.

The Pink Palace Beach Resort
The Pink Palace Beach Resort is located in the village of Agios Gordios on the west coast of the island and offers both hostel-style dormitory rooms and private rooms. The dorms accommodate up to 10 people, while the private rooms offer a more comfortable and private stay.

The Pink Palace Beach Resort has a range of facilities, including a swimming pool, private beach access, and a restaurant and bar. The resort also offers a range of activities and tours, including hiking, kayaking, and snorkeling trips.

The Grapevine Hostel

The Grapevine Hostel is located in the heart of Corfu Town and offers both dormitory-style and private rooms. The dorms accommodate up to six people, while the private rooms offer a more comfortable and private stay.

The Grapevine Hostel has a range of facilities, including a communal kitchen and lounge area, as well as a rooftop terrace with stunning views of the town and sea. The hostel also organizes regular events and activities, including wine tastings, city tours, and pub crawls.

Overall, hostels are a great budget-friendly accommodation option for those looking to socialize and make new friends while exploring all that Corfu has to offer. With a range of facilities and activities on offer, travelers are sure to have a memorable stay at any of the hostels on the island.

Agnes Rooms and Hostel

Agnes Rooms and Hostel is located in the village of Paleokastritsa on the west coast of the island and offers budget-friendly accommodation in both dormitory-style and private rooms. The dorms accommodate up to six people, while the private rooms offer a more comfortable and private stay.

Agnes Rooms and Hostel has a range of facilities, including a communal kitchen and outdoor terrace, as well as a lounge area with a TV and games. The hostel also organizes regular activities and events, including BBQs, karaoke nights, and live music.

The Lazy Bay Hostel

The Lazy Bay Hostel is located in the village of Paleokastritsa on the west coast of the island and offers both dormitory-style and private rooms. The dorms accommodate up to six people, while the private rooms offer a more comfortable and private stay.

The Lazy Bay Hostel has a range of facilities, including a communal kitchen and outdoor terrace, as well as a lounge area with a TV and games. The hostel also organizes regular activities and events, including movie nights, BBQs, and pub crawls.

Overall, hostels in Corfu offer budget-friendly accommodation options for travelers who are looking for a social atmosphere and a range of facilities and activities. With several options available throughout the island, guests are sure to find the perfect hostel for their needs and budget.

Guesthouses

Guesthouses are a unique type of accommodation that provides visitors with an opportunity to experience local culture and hospitality. These properties are typically small, family-run establishments that offer a more personalized and intimate experience than traditional hotels. Corfu has several guesthouses, each with its own unique charm and character.

Villa Karmar

Villa Karmar, located in the village of Agios Gordios on the west coast of the island, is a popular guesthouse option. This property is surrounded by lush greenery and offers stunning views of the sea and the surrounding countryside. Villa Karmar offers several apartments and studios, each featuring a kitchenette and a balcony or terrace with views of the sea or the garden. The rooms are spacious and tastefully decorated, with traditional Greek touches such as colorful tiles and wooden furniture.

The guesthouse has a swimming pool, sun loungers, and a shaded terrace where guests can relax and enjoy the beautiful views. There is also a barbecue area for guests to use. The property is within walking distance of several beaches and traditional Greek tavernas, making it an ideal base for exploring the island.

Villa Anthemia

Villa Anthemia, located in the village of Liapades on the west coast of the island, is another popular guesthouse option. This property is set in a beautiful garden with fruit trees and flowers and offers stunning views of the sea and the surrounding countryside. Villa Anthemia offers several apartments and studios, each featuring a kitchenette and a balcony or terrace with views of the sea or the garden. The rooms are decorated in a traditional Greek style, with colorful tiles and wooden furniture.

The guesthouse has a swimming pool and a shaded terrace where guests can relax and enjoy the beautiful views. There is also a barbecue area for guests to use. The property is within walking distance of several beaches and traditional Greek tavernas, making it an ideal base for exploring the island.

Villa Deza

Villa Deza, located in the village of Agios Georgios on the north-west coast of the island, is a charming guesthouse that offers visitors a tranquil and relaxing retreat. The property is set in a peaceful garden with olive and fruit trees and offers stunning views of the sea and the surrounding countryside. Villa Deza offers several apartments and studios, each featuring a kitchenette and a balcony or terrace with views of the sea or the garden. The rooms are decorated in a traditional Greek style, with wooden furniture and colorful textiles.

The guesthouse has a swimming pool, sun loungers, and a shaded terrace where guests can relax and enjoy the beautiful views. There is also a barbecue area for guests to use. The property is within walking distance of several beaches and traditional Greek tavernas, making it an ideal base for exploring the island.

Villa Makris

Villa Makris, located in the village of Pelekas on the west coast of the island, is another budget-friendly guesthouse option in Corfu. The property is set in a beautiful garden with olive trees and offers stunning views of the sea and the surrounding countryside. Villa Makris offers several apartments and studios, each featuring a kitchenette and a balcony or terrace with views of the sea or the garden. The rooms are decorated in a traditional Greek style, with wooden furniture and colorful textiles.

The guesthouse has a swimming pool and a shaded terrace where guests can relax and enjoy the beautiful views. There is also a barbecue area for guests to use. The property is within walking distance of several beaches and traditional Greek tavernas, making it an ideal base for exploring the island.

Pension Egrypos

Pension Egrypos, located in the village of Benitses on the east coast of the island, is a family-run guesthouse that offers a cozy and welcoming atmosphere. The property is set in a peaceful garden and offers stunning views of the sea and the surrounding countryside. Pension Egrypos offers several rooms and apartments, each featuring a kitchenette and a balcony or terrace with views of the sea or the garden. The rooms are decorated in a traditional Greek style, with wooden furniture and colorful textiles.

The guesthouse has a swimming pool and a shaded terrace where guests can relax and enjoy the beautiful views. There is also a barbecue area for guests to use. The property is within walking distance of several beaches and traditional Greek tavernas, making it an ideal base for exploring the island.

The Lido Sofia Apartments

The Lido Sofia Apartments, located in the village of Gouvia on the east coast of the island, is another budget-friendly guesthouse option in Corfu. The property is set in a peaceful garden and offers stunning views of the sea and the surrounding countryside. The Lido Sofia Apartments offers several apartments, each featuring a kitchenette and a balcony or terrace with views of the sea or the garden. The rooms are decorated in a traditional Greek style, with wooden furniture and colorful textiles.

The guesthouse has a swimming pool and a shaded terrace where guests can relax and enjoy the beautiful views. There is also a barbecue area for guests to use. The property is within walking distance of several beaches and traditional Greek tavernas, making it an ideal base for exploring the island.

Overall, budget-friendly guesthouses in Corfu offer visitors a unique and authentic Greek experience without breaking the bank. Whether you choose Villa Makris, Pension Egrypos, or The Lido Sofia Apartments, you're sure to enjoy a memorable stay in one of these charming and welcoming guesthouses.

Self-Catering Apartments

Self-catering apartments are another great budget-friendly option in Corfu, particularly for families or groups of travelers who want more space and privacy than a hostel or budget hotel can offer.

The Helena Apartments, located in the village of Gouvia on the east coast of the island, is a popular self-catering apartment option. This property offers several apartments and studios, each featuring a kitchenette and balcony or terrace with views of the surrounding gardens or the sea. The apartments also have a swimming pool and are within walking distance of several restaurants and supermarkets.

Another self-catering apartment option is the Levant Hotel & Apartments, located in the village of Agios Gordios on the west coast of the island. This property offers several apartments and studios, each featuring a kitchenette and balcony or terrace with views of the sea or the surrounding countryside. The apartments also have access to a swimming pool and are within walking distance of several beaches and restaurants.

Camping

For adventurous travelers who want to experience the natural beauty of Corfu without breaking the bank, camping is a great option. There are several campsites on the island, offering visitors the chance to stay in a tent or camper van and explore the island's beaches and countryside.

One popular camping option in Corfu is the Camping Paleokastritsa, located in the village of Paleokastritsa on the west coast of the island. This campsite offers several tent pitches and camper van spots, as well as a range of facilities including a swimming pool, restaurant, and laundry facilities. The campsite is also located within walking distance of several beaches and hiking trails.

Another popular camping option is the Corfu Camping, located in the village of Dassia on the east coast of the island. This campsite offers tent pitches, camper van spots, and bungalows, as well as a range of facilities including a swimming pool, restaurant, and mini-market. The campsite is also located within walking distance of several beaches and restaurants.

Overall, Corfu offers a wide range of budget-friendly accommodation options, from budget hotels and hostels to self-catering apartments and camping. Whether you're a backpacker, a family on a budget, or a traveler seeking an alternative to traditional hotels, there is an affordable and comfortable accommodation option for you on this beautiful Greek island.

In conclusion, Corfu offers a wide range of accommodation options to suit every budget and preference. Whether you're seeking a luxurious beachfront resort or a budget-friendly hostel, you're sure to find the perfect place to stay on this beautiful Greek island.

CHAPTER FOUR

ATTRACTIONS AND ACTIVITIES IN CORFU

Corfu, a stunning Greek island in the Ionian Sea, offers a wide array of captivating attractions and activities. From pristine beaches with crystal-clear waters to historical landmarks steeped in rich history, Corfu has something for everyone. Explore charming villages, indulge in delicious Greek cuisine, visit ancient ruins, and bask in the island's natural beauty. Here are some of the attractions and activities to engage in for that Corfu experience feeling

Beaches

Corfu is home to some of the most beautiful beaches in Greece. One of the biggest draws of Corfu is its stunning beaches. With a wide variety of beaches to choose from, visitors can find a beach that suits their needs, whether they want a quiet and secluded cove or a lively beach with plenty of activities. Here are some of the best beaches in Corfu:

Glyfada Beach

Located on the west coast of the island, Glyfada Beach is one of Corfu's most popular beaches. This beautiful stretch of coastline features soft golden sand, crystal-clear waters, and stunning views of the surrounding hills. The beach is approximately 16 kilometers from Corfu Town and can be easily reached by car or bus.

Glyfada Beach is a well-developed beach and offers visitors a range of beachside amenities, including sun loungers, umbrellas, showers, and changing rooms. There are also several beachside bars and restaurants where you can enjoy a refreshing drink or a delicious meal while taking in the beautiful views.

For those looking for some adventure, there are plenty of water sports available at Glyfada Beach, including jet skiing, parasailing, and banana boat rides. The beach is also a great spot for snorkeling, as the waters are teeming with marine life.

In addition to its beautiful beach, Glyfada is surrounded by lush greenery, making it an ideal spot for nature lovers. There are several hiking trails in the area, including a scenic coastal path that offers stunning views of the Ionian Sea.

Glyfada Beach is particularly popular with families, as the shallow waters and soft sand make it a safe and enjoyable spot for children. There is also a children's playground located near the beach, as well as several kid-friendly activities, including mini golf and go-karting.

Overall, Glyfada Beach is a must-visit destination for anyone traveling to Corfu. With its beautiful scenery, range of amenities, and activities, there is something for everyone to enjoy.

Sidari Beach

Sidari Beach is located on the northern coast of Corfu, approximately 40 kilometers from Corfu Town. It is a long, sandy beach with crystal-clear waters and stunning rock formations, making it a popular destination for tourists. The beach is also known for its lively atmosphere and numerous beachside amenities, including sun loungers, umbrellas, and water sports equipment.

One of the most famous rock formations on the beach is the Canal d'Amour, which is believed to have mystical properties. The Canal d'Amour is a natural formation of sandstone cliffs that have been shaped by the sea over millions of years. The formation features several small coves and inlets that are perfect for swimming, snorkeling, and exploring.

In addition to the beach and rock formations, Sidari has plenty of activities and attractions for visitors. One of the most popular things to do is to take a boat tour around the coastline, which allows visitors to see the beach and rock formations from a different perspective. There are also several bars and restaurants along the beachfront, making it a great place to relax and enjoy a meal or a drink.

For those who prefer to stay active, there are plenty of water sports activities available at Sidari Beach, including jet skiing, parasailing, and banana boating. Visitors can also rent a kayak or paddleboard to explore the coastline on their own.

Overall, Sidari Beach is a must-visit destination for anyone traveling to Corfu. Its stunning rock formations, crystal-clear waters, and lively atmosphere make it a perfect place to spend a day or two exploring and relaxing.

Paleokastritsa Beach
Paleokastritsa Beach is located on the northwest coast of the island and is one of the most beautiful beaches in Corfu. The beach is surrounded by steep cliffs and is known for its crystal-clear waters and picturesque scenery.

The beach is actually made up of several small coves, each with its own unique charm. Visitors can explore the coves by renting a boat or taking a guided tour. The water is warm and inviting, making it the perfect place for swimming, snorkeling, and other water sports.

In addition to its natural beauty, Paleokastritsa is also home to several restaurants, cafes, and shops. Visitors can enjoy a delicious meal or snack while taking in the stunning views of the beach and surrounding cliffs.

One of the most popular attractions in Paleokastritsa is the Monastery of the Virgin Mary, which is located on a hill overlooking the beach. The monastery was built in the 13th century and features beautiful Byzantine architecture and stunning views of the surrounding countryside.

For those looking for a more active experience, there are several hiking trails in the area that offer stunning views of the beach and surrounding landscape. One of the most popular trails leads to the nearby Angelokastro Fortress, which was built in the 13th century and offers panoramic views of the surrounding area.

Overall, Paleokastritsa Beach is a must-visit destination for anyone traveling to Corfu. Its natural beauty, clear waters, and rich history make it a truly unforgettable experience.

Agios Gordios Beach

Agios Gordios Beach is one of the most beautiful and popular beaches in Corfu. Located on the west coast of the island, about 15 kilometers from Corfu

Town, the beach stretches for about 1.5 kilometers and offers soft golden sand and crystal-clear waters. The beach is a popular destination for both tourists and locals, thanks to its natural beauty and range of amenities.

Visitors to Agios Gordios Beach can rent sun loungers and umbrellas, as well as enjoy a range of water sports activities such as windsurfing, kayaking, and parasailing. The beach is also popular for swimming, with the water being calm and shallow in some parts. The beach is surrounded by cliffs and lush greenery, offering visitors a picturesque and peaceful setting for a day out.

There are also several beachside restaurants and bars that serve refreshments and snacks throughout the day, making it easy to spend the whole day at the beach. Visitors can enjoy traditional Greek dishes such as fresh seafood, grilled meats, and Greek salads, as well as international cuisine. The beach bars offer a range of drinks and cocktails, making it a great spot to enjoy a refreshing drink while soaking up the sun.

Agios Gordios is also a great base for exploring the surrounding area. Visitors can take a short walk to the nearby village of the same name, which is known for its traditional architecture and narrow streets. There are several shops and cafes in the village, offering visitors a chance to explore the local culture and cuisine. The nearby Agios Gordios cliffs offer spectacular views of the Ionian Sea, and visitors can take a walk along the cliff path to admire the natural beauty of the area.

Overall, Agios Gordios Beach is a must-visit destination for anyone visiting Corfu. With its stunning natural beauty, range of amenities, and proximity to the charming village and beautiful cliffs, it offers visitors a chance to experience the best of Corfu's culture and natural beauty.

Kassiopi Beach

Kassiopi Beach is a beautiful pebble beach located on the northeast coast of Corfu, approximately 38 kilometers from Corfu Town. This stunning beach is a popular destination for families and couples who are looking for a peaceful and relaxed atmosphere. The beach is known for its crystal-clear waters, perfect for swimming, snorkeling, and other water activities.

Kassiopi Beach is surrounded by lush green hills, which provide a stunning backdrop for visitors as they enjoy the beach. There are plenty of facilities available on the beach, including sun loungers, umbrellas, and showers. Visitors can also rent equipment for water sports, such as paddleboards and pedal boats.

In addition to the beach, visitors can explore the charming village of Kassiopi, located just a short walk from the beach. The village has a picturesque harbor with fishing boats and yachts, as well as a range of shops, cafes, and restaurants. Visitors can wander through the narrow streets of the village, exploring the local markets and admiring the traditional architecture.

For those interested in history, the ruins of the ancient Roman baths are located just a short distance from Kassiopi Beach. The baths were built in the 2nd century AD and were used as a place for relaxation and socializing. Visitors can explore the ruins and learn more about the history of the area.

Overall, Kassiopi Beach is a beautiful and tranquil destination that is perfect for those looking to escape the crowds and enjoy a peaceful day by the sea. With plenty of facilities and activities available, visitors are sure to have a memorable time on this stunning beach.

Kontogialos Beach

Kontogialos Beach is located on the west coast of the island, near the village of Pelekas. The beach is known for its golden sand and crystal-clear waters, and it's surrounded by steep cliffs and lush greenery, offering a picturesque backdrop for sunbathing and swimming. Visitors can rent sun loungers and umbrellas, as well as enjoy a range of water sports activities such as windsurfing and paddleboarding. There are also several beachside restaurants and bars that serve refreshments and snacks throughout the day.

Issos Beach

Issos Beach is located on the southwest coast of the island, near the village of Agios Georgios. The beach is known for its unique landscape, as it's situated between two sand dunes that separate the sea from the Lake Korission, a protected wetland area. The beach is ideal for walking and exploring, as well as swimming and sunbathing. Visitors can rent sun loungers and umbrellas, as well as enjoy a range of water sports activities such as kiteboarding and windsurfing. There are also several beachside restaurants and bars that serve refreshments and snacks throughout the day.

Myrtiotissa Beach

Myrtiotissa Beach is located on the west coast of the island, near the village of Vatos. The beach is known for its stunning beauty, as it's surrounded by steep cliffs covered in greenery, offering a secluded and peaceful atmosphere. The beach is popular with naturists, but it's also suitable for visitors who prefer to wear swimsuits. The water is crystal-clear and perfect for swimming and snorkeling. Visitors can rent sun loungers and umbrellas, as well as enjoy a range of water sports activities such as paddleboarding and kayaking.

Overall, Corfu offers an abundance of stunning beaches that cater to all kinds of visitors. Whether you're looking for a peaceful and secluded spot to relax, or an active beach with plenty of water sports activities, you'll find a beach that suits your needs on this beautiful island.

Historical Sites

Corfu has a rich history and is home to several historical sites that are well worth a visit. Some of the most popular historical sites include:

Old Fortress

The Old Fortress, also known as the Venetian Fortress, is a historic castle located on a rocky promontory on the eastern end of Corfu Town. The fortress was built by the Venetians in the 15th century to protect the island from Ottoman attacks, and it has since played an important role in the island's history.

The fortress is accessed through a stone bridge that connects it to the mainland, and visitors can explore its impressive walls and towers, which offer panoramic views of the sea and the town. The fortress is a popular spot for taking photographs, especially during sunset.

Inside the fortress, visitors can explore a number of historic buildings, including the British barracks and the Venetian prison. The prison, which has now been converted into a museum, is a must-visit for anyone interested in the history of the fortress. The museum features exhibits on the history of the fortress and the island, as well as displays of weapons, armor, and other artifacts from the Venetian period.

Visitors can also explore the fortress's interior, which includes a network of tunnels and underground chambers. The tunnels were used by the Venetians as a means of escaping from the fortress in the event of an attack, and they are now open to the public for guided tours.

In addition to its historical significance, the Old Fortress is also a popular venue for cultural events and performances. During the summer months, the fortress hosts concerts, theater performances, and other cultural events, which draw large crowds of locals and tourists alike.

Overall, the Old Fortress is a must-visit for anyone interested in history or architecture, and its stunning location and impressive structures make it one of the most iconic landmarks in Corfu.

Palace of St. Michael and St. George

The Palace of St. Michael and St. George is a grand neoclassical building located in the heart of Corfu Town. The building was constructed between 1819 and 1824 during the British Protectorate of the Ionian Islands, serving as a residence for the British High Commissioner. It was designed by Sir George Whitmore, who was the chief architect of the British Empire.

The palace has an impressive facade with three floors and a central colonnade, flanked by two symmetrical wings. The facade is decorated with sculptures and reliefs of ancient Greek and Roman figures, and the palace's main entrance is a grand arched doorway with Corinthian columns.

Today, the palace houses two museums: the Museum of Asian Art and the Museum of Byzantine Art.

Museum of Asian Art

The Museum of Asian Art is one of the largest and most important collections of Asian art in Europe. The museum was established in 1928 and is housed on the first floor of the palace.

The museum's collection consists of over 10,000 objects, ranging from ancient Chinese bronzes to contemporary Japanese prints. The exhibits are arranged by country and period, and visitors can see a wide variety of art and artifacts, including ceramics, sculptures, paintings, textiles, and metalwork.

Some of the highlights of the collection include a set of Chinese imperial jade carvings, a collection of Korean celadon ceramics, and a number of important Indian miniature paintings. The museum also has a library of over 10,000 books and manuscripts related to Asian art and culture.

Museum of Byzantine Art
The Museum of Byzantine Art is located on the ground floor of the palace and houses a collection of Byzantine and post-Byzantine art from the 4th to the 19th century.

The collection includes icons, frescoes, mosaics, and other religious art, as well as secular objects such as jewelry, coins, and textiles. The exhibits are arranged chronologically and thematically, tracing the development of Byzantine art and its influence on later periods.

Some of the highlights of the collection include a 6th-century mosaic of the Madonna and Child, a 12th-century icon of St. George, and a 16th-century embroidered altar cloth. The museum also has a library with over 5,000 books and manuscripts related to Byzantine art and history.

Visitors to the Palace of St. Michael and St. George can purchase a combined ticket that allows access to both museums. The palace is open to visitors from Tuesday to Sunday, and guided tours are available.

Achilleion Palace

The Achilleion Palace is a beautiful neoclassical palace that was built by the Empress Elisabeth of Austria, also known as Sisi, in the late 19th century. The palace is located in the village of Gastouri, about 10 kilometers south of Corfu Town, and it is one of the most popular tourist attractions on the island.

The palace was designed by the Italian architect Raffaele Caritto, and it is inspired by the mythical hero Achilles, who was said to have been born on the island of Corfu. The palace is adorned with sculptures and frescoes that depict scenes from Greek mythology, and it is surrounded by beautiful gardens that offer stunning views of the surrounding countryside.

Visitors to the palace can explore the ornate rooms, which are decorated with marble floors, crystal chandeliers, and beautiful frescoes. One of the most famous rooms in the palace is the Sisi Museum, which is dedicated to the life and legacy of Empress Elisabeth.

The museum features exhibits on Sisi's personal life, including her hobbies, her travels, and her political interests. Visitors can see her personal items, such as her jewelry, her dresses, and her personal belongings, and they can learn about her tragic death.

Another famous feature of the palace is the statue of Achilles that stands in the palace gardens. The statue depicts the legendary Greek hero in full armor, with his sword and shield, and it is a popular photo spot for visitors.

In addition to the palace and gardens, visitors can also explore the village of Gastouri, which has a traditional Corfiot feel. The village has a number of cafes and restaurants where visitors can sample local cuisine, and there are also several shops where visitors can buy souvenirs and handicrafts.

Overall, the Achilleion Palace is a must-visit for anyone interested in history, art, or architecture. The palace is a stunning example of neoclassical design, and it offers a fascinating glimpse into the life of one of Europe's most famous royal figures.

Mon Repos Palace

Mon Repos Palace is a beautiful neoclassical villa located in a verdant parkland in the Kanoni area, about 3 kilometers south of Corfu Town. The palace was built by the British in the late 19th century as a summer residence for the high commissioner of the Ionian Islands.

The palace is surrounded by lush gardens, which are home to a variety of exotic plants and trees, as well as several ancient ruins. Visitors can explore the palace's interior, which has been preserved in its original state, and admire the beautiful frescoes and furnishings.

The villa was later used as a royal residence, and it was the birthplace of Prince Philip, Duke of Edinburgh, in 1921. The villa and its gardens are now open to the public as a museum and a popular tourist attraction.

Inside the villa, visitors can explore the elegant rooms, which are filled with antique furniture, artwork, and other historic artifacts. The rooms are decorated in a neoclassical style, with marble floors, ornate ceilings, and beautiful frescoes.

One of the highlights of the villa is the room where Prince Philip was born, which has been preserved in its original state. Visitors can see the simple wooden crib where the future Duke of Edinburgh slept as a baby, as well as other personal items and photographs.

Outside the villa, the gardens are a beautiful oasis of greenery, dotted with ancient ruins and sculptures.

Visitors can stroll along the winding paths, enjoying the shade of the trees and the scent of the flowers. One of the most impressive features of the gardens is the ancient Greek temple of Hera, which was moved to the site from a nearby location in the 19th century.

Overall, Mon Repos Palace is a must-visit for anyone interested in history, art, or architecture. The villa and its gardens offer a glimpse into the luxurious lifestyle of the British elite in the 19th century, as well as a fascinating insight into the island's rich cultural heritage.

Kassiopi Castle

Kassiopi Castle is located in the picturesque village of Kassiopi on the northeast coast of Corfu. The castle is a well-preserved example of medieval military architecture, and it offers stunning views of the Ionian Sea and the surrounding countryside.

The castle was built by the Byzantines in the 13th century as part of a defensive network to protect the island from pirate raids. Later on, it was occupied by the Venetians and the British. In the 16th century, the castle was expanded by the Venetians to include a large tower and a series of bastions.

Visitors to Kassiopi Castle can explore the castle's walls and towers, which offer panoramic views of the sea and the village below. The castle's interior is now in ruins, but visitors can still see the remains of the Venetian tower and the fortress's walls, which are adorned with various crests and emblems.

In addition to the castle itself, visitors to Kassiopi can also explore the village's charming harbor and stroll along the seafront promenade. The village is known for its lively atmosphere, and visitors can enjoy a variety of shops, restaurants, and cafes.

Kassiopi is also a popular spot for swimming and snorkeling, with several beaches and coves located nearby. The most popular beach in Kassiopi is Kalamionas, a pebbly beach with crystal-clear water, which is located just a short walk from the castle.

Overall, Kassiopi Castle is a fascinating historical site and a must-visit for anyone interested in medieval architecture and military history. Whether you're exploring the castle's ruins or soaking up the village's lively atmosphere, Kassiopi is a highlight of any trip to Corfu.

Angelokastro Fortress
Angelokastro Fortress, also known as the Castle of the Angels, is one of the most impressive historical sites in Corfu. The fortress is located on a steep hilltop, about 25 kilometers from Corfu Town, and was built in the 13th century by the Byzantines to protect the island from invaders.

The fortress is situated at an altitude of 305 meters above sea level, and the climb to the top can be quite steep and strenuous, but the breathtaking views of the surrounding countryside and the Ionian Sea make it well worth the effort. The fortress is surrounded by lush vegetation, including olive groves, cypress trees, and wildflowers, which add to the beauty of the site.

The fortress itself is made up of a series of walls and towers, which were built using the natural stone of the hill. The walls are up to 2.5 meters thick in some places, and the towers offer stunning panoramic views of the coastline.

Inside the fortress, visitors can explore the ruins of the ancient buildings, including the main tower, which is the highest point of the fortress. The tower offers a 360-degree view of the island, and on a clear day, visitors can see as far as the Greek mainland.

In addition to the tower, visitors can also explore the remains of the cisterns, the barracks, and the dungeons. The cisterns were used to store water for the fortress's inhabitants, and visitors can still see the ancient aqueducts that brought water to the site.

The barracks were used to house the soldiers who defended the fortress, and visitors can see the remains of the sleeping quarters, the kitchen, and the storage rooms. The dungeons were used to hold prisoners, and visitors can still see the remains of the cells and the torture chamber.

Overall, Angelokastro Fortress is a fascinating and impressive historical site, and a must-visit for anyone interested in medieval history and architecture. The site offers stunning views, ancient ruins, and a glimpse into the island's rich and fascinating history.

Corfu Old Town
Corfu Old Town is the historic center of Corfu and a UNESCO World Heritage Site. It is one of the best-preserved medieval towns in Greece and a must-visit for anyone interested in history and architecture.

The old town is a maze of narrow streets and alleyways, lined with colorful buildings, ancient churches, and historic landmarks. Visitors can easily spend a full day exploring its many treasures, including:

Liston: This elegant arcade is one of the most popular spots in the old town. It was built during the French occupation in the early 19th century and is now lined with cafes and restaurants. Visitors can enjoy a cup of coffee or a meal while watching the world go by.

Spianada: This is the largest square in the Balkans and a popular gathering place for locals and tourists alike. The square is surrounded by historic buildings, including the Palace of St. Michael and St. George and the Old Fortress.

Old Fortress: The fortress is located at the eastern end of Corfu Old Town and was built by the Venetians in the 15th century. Visitors can explore the fortress's walls and towers and enjoy stunning views of the town and the sea.

New Fortress: The fortress was built by the Venetians in the 16th century to protect the town from invading Ottoman forces. It is located on a hill overlooking the old town and offers breathtaking views of the surrounding countryside.

Saint Spyridon Church: This is the most important church in Corfu and the final resting place of Saint Spyridon, the island's patron saint. The church features a beautiful bell tower and stunning frescoes.

Jewish Quarter: The Jewish Quarter is located in the heart of Corfu Old Town and features several historic synagogues and museums. Visitors can learn about the rich history of Corfu's Jewish community and explore its many treasures.

Other highlights of Corfu Old Town include the Venetian-style buildings, the ancient churches, and the many artisan shops selling traditional Corfiot products such as olive oil, honey, and wine.

Overall, Corfu Old Town is a fascinating mix of Venetian, French, and British architecture, and a must-visit for anyone interested in history, culture, and architecture.

In conclusion, Corfu is a treasure trove of historical sites, and visitors can spend days exploring the island's many castles, palaces, and ancient ruins. Whether you're a history buff or simply looking to soak up some culture, Corfu has something to offer everyone.

Museums

Corfu is home to several museums that are well worth a visit. Some of the most popular museums include:

Archaeological Museum

The Archaeological Museum of Corfu is a must-visit destination for anyone interested in the history and culture of ancient Greece. The museum is located in the historic Palace of Saint Michael and Saint George in the heart of Corfu Town, and its exhibits cover a wide range of periods, from the prehistoric era to the Roman period.

One of the highlights of the museum is the Gorgon pediment, which is a large stone slab carved with a scene from Greek mythology. The pediment was originally part of the Temple of Artemis in Corfu and dates back to the 6th century BC. The carving depicts the Gorgon Medusa with her hair made of snakes and her eyes staring out fiercely. The pediment is considered one of the finest examples of ancient Greek sculpture and is a stunning piece of art to behold.

The museum's collection also includes a large number of artifacts from the ancient city of Corfu, including pottery, sculpture, inscriptions, and funerary offerings. One of the most interesting exhibits is a collection of figurines of the Tanagra type, which were produced in Boeotia in the 4th and 3rd centuries BC. These figurines depict women and men engaged in various activities, such as playing musical instruments or participating in athletic competitions.

Another highlight of the museum is the collection of Roman marble statues, which were found in the Palace of the Roman Governor in Corfu. These statues depict Roman emperors, goddesses, and other figures, and offer a glimpse into the art and culture of the Roman Empire.

In addition to its exhibits, the Archaeological Museum of Corfu also has a beautiful garden with sculptures and a café where visitors can relax and enjoy a cup of coffee or a snack. The museum is open daily, except on Mondays, and admission is affordable. Guided tours are also available for those who want to learn more about the museum's exhibits and the history of Corfu.

Museum of Asian Art

The Museum of Asian Art, also known as the Asian Art Museum of Corfu, is a fascinating museum that showcases a wide range of art and artifacts from Asia. It is one of the most important museums of its kind in Greece and attracts visitors from all over the world.

The museum was established in 1928 by the Greek diplomat Gregorios Manos, who was an avid collector of Asian art. Manos traveled extensively throughout Asia, collecting art and artifacts from countries such as China, Japan, India, and Southeast Asia. He brought his collection back to Greece and donated it to the state, along with funds to create a museum to house it.

Today, the Museum of Asian Art is housed in the Palace of Saint Michael and Saint George in Corfu Town, which is an impressive neoclassical building that was constructed in the early 19th century. The museum's collection includes over 10,000 items, ranging from paintings and ceramics to textiles and metalwork. The exhibits cover a time period from the Neolithic era to the 19th century, and they offer a fascinating glimpse into the rich cultural heritage of Asia.

One of the most impressive items in the collection is the 3-meter-high Japanese Buddha statue made of lacquered wood, which is located in the central hall of the museum. The statue is intricately carved and is adorned with gold leaf and precious stones. Other highlights of the collection include Chinese porcelain vases, Indian miniature paintings, and Japanese samurai swords.

The museum also hosts temporary exhibitions that showcase different aspects of Asian art and culture. These exhibitions are usually accompanied by lectures and workshops, which offer visitors the opportunity to learn more about the exhibits and the cultures that produced them.

In addition to its impressive collection, the Museum of Asian Art also has a beautiful garden that is open to the public. The garden is filled with sculptures and other works of art, and it offers a peaceful retreat from the hustle and bustle of Corfu Town.

Overall, the Museum of Asian Art is a must-visit destination for anyone interested in Asian art and culture. Its collection is both extensive and impressive, and it offers a unique insight into the rich artistic traditions of Asia.

Solomos Museum

The Solomos Museum is located in the village of Zakynthos, which is about a two-hour ferry ride from Corfu. The museum is dedicated to the life and work of the Greek poet Dionysios Solomos, who is considered to be the national poet of Greece. He wrote the poem "Hymn to Liberty," which later became the national anthem of Greece. The museum is housed in the house where Solomos was born and lived for most of his life, and it offers visitors a unique insight into the life of one of Greece's most beloved poets.

The museum's exhibits include manuscripts, letters, personal belongings, and first editions of Solomos' works. The exhibits are displayed in various rooms of the house, and they are arranged chronologically to give visitors a sense of the poet's life and work. The museum also features audio-visual presentations that provide additional information about Solomos' life and the historical context in which he lived.

One of the highlights of the museum is the room that displays Solomos' original manuscript of "Hymn to Liberty." This manuscript is considered to be one of the most important literary documents in modern Greek history, and it is kept in a specially designed glass case to protect it from damage. Visitors can see the manuscript up close and appreciate the care and attention to detail that went into its creation.

Another interesting exhibit in the museum is a recreation of Solomos' study, which is furnished with period furniture and other personal items. Visitors can see the desk where the poet wrote his works and the bookshelves that held his extensive collection of books. The study provides a glimpse into the poet's daily life and the environment in which he created his masterpieces.

The museum also has a garden that features a bronze statue of Solomos. The statue is surrounded by plants and flowers, and it provides a peaceful and reflective setting for visitors to contemplate the poet's life and work.

In addition to its permanent exhibits, the Solomos Museum also hosts temporary exhibitions, lectures, and cultural events throughout the year. These events showcase the work of contemporary artists and writers and provide visitors with an opportunity to experience the vibrant cultural scene of Zakynthos and Greece as a whole.

Overall, the Solomos Museum is a must-visit destination for anyone interested in Greek literature, history, or culture. The museum's exhibits and beautiful surroundings offer visitors a unique and immersive experience that is sure to leave a lasting impression.

Byzantine Museum

The Byzantine Museum is one of the most important museums in Corfu, showcasing a stunning collection of Byzantine and post-Byzantine art and artifacts. The museum is located in the Church of Antivouniotissa, a beautiful 15th-century church in the heart of Corfu Town.

The museum's exhibits cover a wide range of topics, including religion, history, and art. Visitors can admire a stunning collection of icons, frescoes, manuscripts, and other religious artifacts from the Byzantine and post-Byzantine periods. The exhibits cover a time period from the 13th to the 18th century, offering a glimpse into the rich religious heritage of Corfu.

One of the most impressive items in the museum's collection is the 15th-century icon of the Virgin Mary, which is made of silver and gold and is adorned with precious stones. This icon is considered to be one of the most important works of Byzantine art in Greece and is a must-see for anyone interested in art and history.

Other notable items in the museum's collection include the 16th-century frescoes from the Church of St. Nicholas in Kassiopi, the 14th-century manuscript of the Four Gospels, and the 17th-century icon of Saint Spyridon, the patron saint of Corfu. The museum also features a number of temporary exhibits throughout the year, showcasing various aspects of Byzantine and post-Byzantine art and culture.

In addition to its impressive collection of artifacts, the Byzantine Museum also offers visitors a chance to learn about the history of the Church of Antivouniotissa. The church was built in the 15th century and was dedicated to the Virgin Mary. It features a beautiful interior with intricate frescoes and icons, making it a must-visit for anyone interested in Byzantine architecture and art.

Overall, the Byzantine Museum is a must-visit destination for anyone interested in art, history, and religion. With its impressive collection of artifacts and stunning location, the museum offers visitors a unique insight into the rich cultural heritage of Corfu.

Museum of Banknotes

The Museum of Banknotes is a fascinating museum located in Corfu Town, dedicated to the history of money and the development of the banking system in Greece. It was founded in 1981 by the Bank of Greece and it is housed in a neoclassical building that used to be the headquarters of the Ionian Bank.

The museum's collection includes banknotes, coins, and other monetary objects from different periods in Greek history. The exhibits cover a time period from ancient times to modern days and offer a fascinating insight into the role that money has played in the Greek society over the centuries.

Visitors to the museum can explore the history of Greek money through a series of interactive exhibits, multimedia displays, and informative panels. The museum's collection includes rare and valuable banknotes and coins, some of which date back to the ancient Greek and Roman times.

One of the highlights of the museum is the collection of banknotes and coins from the Greek War of Independence (1821-1832), which played a crucial role in the fight for Greek independence from the Ottoman Empire. Visitors can see banknotes and coins that were used to finance the war effort and played an important role in shaping the modern Greek state.

Another fascinating exhibit is a reconstruction of a 19th-century Greek bank, complete with teller's desks, safes, and other banking equipment. This exhibit gives visitors a sense of what banking was like in Greece during this period.

The museum also has a library with books and documents related to the history of money and banking in Greece, and it offers educational programs and workshops for visitors of all ages.

The Museum of Banknotes is a must-visit for anyone interested in finance, economics, and the history of Greece. It offers a unique and informative experience that is not to be missed during a visit to Corfu. The museum is open from Tuesday to Sunday and admission is free.

Kapodistrias Museum

The Kapodistrias Museum is located in the village of Corfu, which is about 20 km from Corfu Town. The museum is dedicated to the life and work of Ioannis Kapodistrias, who was a politician, diplomat, and the first governor of the modern Greek state. The museum is housed in the house where Kapodistrias was born and lived, and it offers a unique insight into the history of Greece and the political figures that have shaped it.

Ioannis Kapodistrias was born in Corfu in 1776, which was then part of the Republic of Venice. He received his education in Italy and Russia and became a prominent diplomat and statesman. In 1827, he was appointed as the first governor of the newly established Greek state and he played a crucial role in its early years, working to establish the country's infrastructure, economy, and political system.

The Kapodistrias Museum is a small but well-organized museum that showcases the life and work of this important historical figure. The museum's exhibits include personal belongings, documents, and memorabilia related to Kapodistrias' life and work. Visitors can see Kapodistrias' desk, library, and other personal items, as well as documents related to his diplomatic career and his role as the governor of Greece.

The museum is located in a beautiful neoclassical building that used to be the home of Kapodistrias' family. The building has been restored to its original state with period furniture, clothes, and decorations, giving visitors a sense of what life was like in the 18th and 19th centuries. The museum also has a garden with fruit trees and herbs, which Kapodistrias used to cultivate himself.

Visitors to the Kapodistrias Museum can learn about the history of Greece and the role that this important political figure played in shaping the country's early years. The museum's exhibits are informative and well-presented, and visitors can take their time exploring the different rooms and displays. The museum is also surrounded by beautiful scenery, with views of the sea and the mountains, making it a pleasant destination for a day trip outside of Corfu Town.

Casa Parlante

Casa Parlante is one of the most unique and fascinating museums in Corfu. The museum is located in a beautiful neoclassical building in the heart of Corfu Town, and it offers visitors a glimpse into the daily life of a 19th-century Corfiot family.

The museum is set up like a living house museum, where visitors can explore the different rooms of the house and witness scenes from the family's daily life. The exhibits are interactive and they include period furniture, clothing, and decorations, as well as realistic mannequins that represent the family members going about their daily routines.

One of the most interesting features of Casa Parlante is its attention to detail. The museum's creators have gone to great lengths to recreate the atmosphere of a typical Corfiot home in the 19th century, from the smells of the kitchen to the sounds of the children playing in the courtyard. Visitors can watch the family cooking, dining, reading, and even dancing, as they move from room to room.

In addition to the interior of the house, Casa Parlante also has a beautiful garden that visitors can explore. The garden is filled with Mediterranean plants and it is a peaceful oasis in the heart of the busy town. There is also a café on site, where visitors can enjoy a refreshing drink or a snack after their visit.

Casa Parlante is a must-visit museum for anyone interested in history, culture, and architecture. It offers a unique and immersive experience that will transport visitors back in time and help them understand the daily life of a typical Corfiot family in the 19th century. The museum is open daily from 10am to 6pm, and admission fees are reasonable.

In conclusion, these are some of the museums that you can explore during your visit to Corfu. Each museum offers a unique experience that will help you understand the island's rich history and culture. Make sure to check the opening hours and admission fees before you visit, and don't forget to bring your camera and a curious mind!

Nature

Corfu's stunning natural beauty and diverse landscape make it an ideal destination for nature lovers. If you're interested in hiking, swimming, or just taking in the scenery, there is something for everyone to enjoy. Some of the most popular natural attractions in Corfu include:

Mount Pantokrator

Mount Pantokrator is the highest mountain on the island of Corfu, rising to an elevation of 906 meters (2,972 feet). It is situated in the northeastern part of the island, near the village of Strinilas. The mountain is a popular destination for nature lovers and hikers, offering stunning panoramic views of the Ionian Sea and the surrounding landscape.

Visitors can reach the summit of Mount Pantokrator by car or by foot. The road leading to the summit is paved and in good condition, making it accessible for most vehicles. Along the way, visitors will pass through small villages and olive groves, providing an authentic glimpse into rural life on the island.

For those who prefer to hike, there are several trails leading to the summit of Mount Pantokrator, ranging in difficulty from easy to challenging. The most popular trail starts from the village of Old Perithia, which is a well-preserved traditional village located at the foot of the mountain. From there, hikers can follow the trail through pine forests and past small streams, eventually reaching the summit.

Once at the summit, visitors can enjoy stunning views of the surrounding landscape. On clear days, it is possible to see as far as the Albanian coastline and the neighboring island of Paxos. There is also a small chapel at the summit, dedicated to the Transfiguration of Jesus Christ. The chapel dates back to the 17th century and is an important pilgrimage site for Orthodox Christians.

In addition to the stunning views and hiking trails, Mount Pantokrator is also home to a 14th-century monastery. The monastery, dedicated to the Virgin Mary, is one of the oldest and most important religious sites on the island. Visitors can explore the monastery's grounds and admire its beautiful frescoes and iconography.

Overall, Mount Pantokrator is a must-visit destination for anyone traveling to Corfu. Whether you choose to drive to the summit or hike to the top, the stunning views and rich history of the mountain are sure to leave a lasting impression.

Corfu Trail

The Corfu Trail is a 220-kilometer long-distance hiking trail that traverses the entire island of Corfu. The trail is divided into 12 stages, each of which offers a unique glimpse into the island's history, culture, and natural beauty. The Corfu Trail is a popular attraction for hikers and nature lovers, as it takes visitors through some of the most scenic and unspoiled areas of the island.

The trail begins in the village of Kavos on the southern tip of the island and ends in the village of Agios Spyridon on the northern coast. Hikers can choose to do the entire trail or just one or two stages, depending on their fitness level and time constraints. Each stage of the trail covers a distance of 15-25 kilometers and takes between 5-7 hours to complete.

The Corfu Trail is well-marked and maintained, with signposts and markers guiding hikers along the way. The trail passes through a variety of landscapes, including traditional villages, olive groves, pine forests, rocky outcrops, and stunning beaches. Along the way, hikers can enjoy panoramic views of the Ionian Sea, the mainland of Greece, and the surrounding islands.

One of the highlights of the Corfu Trail is the opportunity to explore the island's rich history and culture. The trail passes by several ancient ruins and historic landmarks, including the 13th-century Byzantine castle of Gardiki, the 14th-century monastery of Panagia ton Xenon, and the 18th-century Achilleion Palace.

The Corfu Trail is also a great way to experience the island's flora and fauna. The trail passes through several protected areas, including the Natura 2000 site of Lake Korission, which is home to several rare species of birds, and the Mount Pantokrator area, which is covered in pine forests and is home to several endemic plant species.

Overall, the Corfu Trail is an unforgettable experience for anyone who loves hiking, nature, and adventure. Whether you're a seasoned hiker or a beginner, the Corfu Trail has something for everyone to enjoy. Just make sure to bring plenty of water, sunscreen, and comfortable hiking shoes!

Canal d'Amour

The Canal d'Amour is a unique natural formation located on the northwestern coast of Corfu, near the town of Sidari. The name "Canal d'Amour" translates to "Channel of Love" in French, and the area is steeped in legend and romance.

The Canal d'Amour is a series of sandstone cliffs that have been eroded over time by the sea and wind, forming narrow channels and small coves. The cliffs are covered in lush vegetation and offer a stunning backdrop for swimming and sunbathing. The crystal-clear waters are perfect for snorkeling, and visitors can often spot a variety of marine life, including colorful fish and sea urchins.

The Canal d'Amour is believed to have mystical properties, and legend has it that couples who swim through the canal together will stay together forever. Visitors often try to swim through the narrowest part of the canal, which is only a few meters wide, in the hopes of cementing their love. The area is also a popular spot for weddings and romantic photo shoots.

In addition to swimming and sunbathing, there are several other activities to enjoy at the Canal d'Amour. Visitors can explore the surrounding cliffs on foot, taking in the stunning views of the Ionian Sea and the nearby islands. There are also several cafes and restaurants nearby where visitors can grab a bite to eat or a drink.

The Canal d'Amour is a popular destination for tourists, and it can get quite crowded during peak season. However, if you visit during the off-season or early in the morning, you may be able to enjoy the area in relative peace and quiet. Regardless of when you visit, the Canal d'Amour is a must-see attraction that is sure to leave a lasting impression.

Mount Agios Dikaios

Mount Agios Dikaios is a mountain located in the center of Corfu, offering visitors a chance to explore the island's lush interior. The mountain stands at an altitude of 580 meters and is surrounded by olive groves, traditional villages, and lush forests.

One of the main attractions of Mount Agios Dikaios is the opportunity to hike along its numerous trails. There are several hiking trails of varying difficulty levels that lead visitors through the mountain's beautiful forests, past ancient ruins and churches, and offer breathtaking views of the surrounding countryside. The trails are well marked and maintained, making it easy for visitors to navigate their way around the mountain.

For those looking for a more leisurely way to explore the mountain, there are several villages located along the slopes of Mount Agios Dikaios that offer a glimpse into traditional Corfiot life. The villages are home to charming cobblestone streets, ancient churches, and traditional tavernas serving up delicious local cuisine. Visitors can wander through the streets, admiring the traditional architecture and soaking in the laid-back atmosphere of village life.

Another popular attraction on Mount Agios Dikaios is the Pantokrator Monastery, which is located near the summit of the mountain. The monastery was built in the 14th century and offers visitors a chance to explore its ornate frescoes, stunning Byzantine architecture, and beautiful gardens. From the monastery, visitors can also enjoy stunning panoramic views of the surrounding countryside, including views of the Ionian Sea and the Albanian coast.

Overall, Mount Agios Dikaios offers visitors a chance to explore the natural beauty and traditional culture of Corfu's interior. It doesn't matter if you're an avid hiker or simply looking for a relaxing day trip, the mountain has something for everyone to enjoy.

Aqualand

Aqualand is a water park located in the village of Agios Ioannis, about 10 kilometers west of Corfu Town. The park covers an area of 75,000 square meters and features a wide range of water slides, pools, and attractions. With over 35 different rides, there is something for visitors of all ages and adrenaline levels.

The water park has several sections, including:

- **Kid's Zone:** A dedicated area for young children, featuring small slides, splash pads, and shallow pools. There are also several play areas and water fountains to keep the little ones entertained.

- **Adventure Zone:** This section is designed for older children and features a range of exciting rides, including the "Crazy River," the "Black Hole," and the "Free Fall."

- **Extreme Zone:** For thrill-seekers, the Extreme Zone offers some of the park's most exciting rides, including the "Kamikaze," the "Hydro-tube," and the "Twister."

- **Relax Zone:** If you're looking to take a break from the excitement, the Relax Zone offers a range of pools and lounging areas. There is also a lazy river where visitors can float along and take in the scenery.

In addition to the rides and attractions, Aqualand has several restaurants and cafes where visitors can grab a bite to eat or a drink. There are also several shops selling souvenirs, swimwear, and other items.

Aqualand is open from May to October and can get quite busy during peak season, so it's recommended to arrive early in the day to avoid the crowds. The park is well-maintained, and safety is a top priority, with lifeguards stationed at each attraction.

Overall, Aqualand is a fun-filled day out for families and friends looking to cool off from the heat and enjoy some water-based fun.

In conclusion, Corfu is a nature lover's paradise with an abundance of natural beauty and diverse landscapes to explore. Whether you're interested in hiking, swimming, or just taking in the stunning scenery, there is something for everyone to enjoy on this beautiful island. From the stunning views of Mount Pantokrator to the crystal-clear waters of Glyfada Beach, Corfu's natural attractions are sure to leave a lasting impression on visitors.

Outdoor Activities

Corfu is a paradise for outdoor enthusiasts and adventure seekers. Whether you are interested in water sports, hiking, or horseback riding, there are plenty of activities to keep you entertained. Here are some of the most popular outdoor activities in Corfu:

Water Sports

Corfu is a paradise for water sports enthusiasts, thanks to its crystal-clear waters and ideal wind conditions. From windsurfing and kitesurfing to snorkeling and scuba diving, there are plenty of water activities to keep you entertained. Here are some of the most popular water sports in Corfu:

Windsurfing

Windsurfing is one of the most popular water sports in Corfu, and for good reason. The island's ideal wind conditions, warm waters, and stunning coastline make it a paradise for windsurfing enthusiasts of all levels. Here's what you need to know about windsurfing in Corfu:

Equipment Rental and Lessons

There are several windsurfing centers on the island that offer equipment rental and windsurfing lessons for all levels of experience. If you're a beginner, it's recommended to take a few lessons to learn the basics of windsurfing before heading out on your own. Most windsurfing schools offer group lessons as well as private lessons with experienced instructors. Equipment rental prices vary depending on the season and the center you choose, but you can expect to pay around 30-40 euros per hour for equipment rental.

Best Windsurfing Spots in Corfu

There are several windsurfing spots in Corfu that are popular among locals and tourists alike. Here are some of the best windsurfing spots in Corfu:

Paleokastritsa: This beautiful bay on the west coast of Corfu is known for its crystal-clear waters and steady winds, making it an ideal spot for windsurfing. There are several windsurfing schools located in Paleokastritsa that offer lessons and equipment rental.

Agios Georgios: This long sandy beach on the northwest coast of Corfu is another popular windsurfing spot. The winds here are strong and consistent, and there are several windsurfing centers that offer equipment rental and lessons.

Issos beach: Located on the southwest coast of Corfu, Issos beach is a beautiful sandy beach with shallow waters and ideal wind conditions for windsurfing. There are several windsurfing centers located on the beach that offer equipment rental and lessons.

Halikounas beach: This long sandy beach on the west coast of Corfu is a popular spot for kitesurfing, but it's also a great spot for windsurfing. The winds here are strong and consistent, and there are several windsurfing centers located nearby.

Tips for Windsurfing in Corfu

Here are some tips to help you make the most of your windsurfing experience in Corfu:

Check the wind conditions before heading out: It's important to check the wind conditions before heading out to ensure that they're safe and suitable for your level of experience. Most windsurfing centers will have a daily wind report that you can check before heading out.

Wear appropriate gear: It's important to wear appropriate gear, such as a wetsuit, harness, and life jacket, to ensure your safety and comfort while windsurfing.

Respect the rules and regulations: Make sure to follow the rules and regulations set by the windsurfing center and local authorities. This includes staying within the designated windsurfing area and avoiding areas with swimmers or other water sports activities.

Have fun: Most importantly, have fun and enjoy the beautiful waters and scenery of Corfu while windsurfing. It's a thrilling and exhilarating activity that is sure to leave you with unforgettable memories.

Kitesurfing

Kitesurfing is a thrilling water sport that combines the excitement of wakeboarding, windsurfing, and paragliding. It involves riding a board while being pulled by a large kite through the water. Kitesurfing in Corfu is particularly popular due to the island's ideal wind conditions and warm waters. Here are some more details on kitesurfing in Corfu:

Location: The most popular kitesurfing spots in Corfu are Agios Georgios, Issos beach, and Halikounas beach. These locations offer perfect conditions for both beginners and experienced riders, with consistent winds and relatively flat waters.

Equipment: You can rent kitesurfing equipment at one of the many kitesurfing centers located along the coast of Corfu. The equipment includes a kite, a board, a harness, and a wetsuit. If you're a beginner, it's recommended to take lessons from a certified instructor before attempting to kitesurf on your own.

Lessons: There are several kitesurfing schools on the island that offer lessons for all levels of experience. Beginner lessons usually involve learning how to control the kite on land before moving onto the water. Intermediate and advanced lessons focus on riding techniques, jumping, and tricks. Private lessons are also available for those who prefer a more personalized approach.

Safety: Kitesurfing can be a dangerous sport if not practiced safely. It's essential to follow the safety rules and guidelines provided by the kitesurfing center or instructor. Always check the wind conditions and avoid kitesurfing in offshore winds. Wear a helmet and a life jacket at all times, and make sure to use a safety leash to detach the kite from your body in case of an emergency.

Kitesurfing Events: Corfu hosts several kitesurfing events throughout the year, attracting riders from all over the world. One of the most popular events is the "Kiteboard Tour Asia," which takes place in Halikounas beach every summer. This event includes races, freestyle competitions, and exhibitions from some of the world's top kitesurfers.

Overall, kitesurfing is an exhilarating water sport that offers a unique way to explore Corfu's stunning coastline. With its ideal wind conditions and warm waters, Corfu is a popular destination for kitesurfing enthusiasts of all levels of experience. Whether you're a beginner or an experienced rider, don't miss the opportunity to try kitesurfing in Corfu.

Sailing

Sailing is a popular outdoor activity in Corfu, and for good reason. The island's stunning coastline, crystal-clear waters, and ideal wind conditions make it the perfect destination for sailing enthusiasts. Whether you're an experienced sailor or a beginner, there are plenty of options available for you to enjoy sailing in Corfu.

One of the best ways to experience sailing in Corfu is to rent a sailboat and explore the island's pristine beaches and secluded coves at your own pace. There are several companies on the island that offer sailboat rentals, from small boats to luxury yachts. If you're new to sailing, you can also hire a skipper to guide you and help you navigate the waters.

If you're looking for a more structured sailing experience, there are several guided sailing tours available on the island. These tours usually last for a full day or half a day, and take you to some of the most beautiful spots around Corfu, including the small islands of Paxos and Antipaxos. These tours are a great way to explore the island's coastline and learn more about the local history and culture.

For those who want to learn how to sail, there are several sailing schools on the island that offer courses for beginners as well as advanced sailors. These courses typically last for a few days and include both theory and practical lessons. By the end of the course, you should have the knowledge and skills necessary to confidently sail a boat on your own.

Finally, for the more adventurous sailors, there are several sailing regattas and races held on the island throughout the year. These events attract sailors from all over the world and offer a unique opportunity to test your skills and compete against other sailors in a friendly and exciting environment.

Overall, sailing is a great way to explore Corfu's beautiful coastline and hidden coves. You can rent a sailboat or join a guided sailing tour and explore the island's pristine beaches and crystal-clear waters. The most popular sailing spots in Corfu are Paleokastritsa, Benitses, and the small islands of Paxos and Antipaxos. There are several sailing centers on the island that offer sailing lessons and charters for all levels of experience. If you're new to sailing, it's recommended to take a few lessons with a certified instructor to learn the basics and ensure your safety.

Water Skiing and Wakeboarding
Water skiing and wakeboarding are two adrenaline-pumping water sports that are popular in Corfu. Several water sports centers on the island offer water skiing and wakeboarding lessons for all levels of experience.

The most popular water skiing and wakeboarding spots in Corfu are Kontokali Bay, Gouvia Bay, and Kassiopi. These beaches offer calm and clear waters, ideal for water skiing and wakeboarding enthusiasts of all levels. If you're new to these sports, it's recommended to take a few lessons with a certified instructor to learn the basics and ensure your safety.

Kayaking and Paddleboarding
Kayaking and paddleboarding are two relaxing water activities that are perfect for those who want to explore Corfu's beautiful coastline at their own pace. You can rent a kayak or a paddleboard and explore the island's hidden coves and secluded beaches.
The most popular kayaking and paddleboarding spots in Corfu are Paleokastritsa, Agni Bay, and Nissaki Bay. These beaches offer calm and clear waters, ideal for kayaking and paddleboarding enthusiasts of all levels.

Snorkeling and Scuba Diving

Corfu's underwater world is home to a variety of marine life and interesting dive sites. There are several diving schools on the island that offer courses for beginners as well as guided dives for experienced divers.

The most popular dive sites in Corfu are the Blue Hole in Paleokastritsa, the Agios Georgios reef, and the submerged plane wreck in Kassiopi. These dive sites offer an exciting and unique underwater experience for divers of all levels. If you're new to diving, it's recommended to take a beginner's course with a certified instructor to learn the basics and ensure your safety. Snorkeling is also a popular activity in Corfu, as the island's clear waters offer great visibility and a chance to see a variety of marine life up close. Some popular snorkeling spots in Corfu include Paleokastritsa, Kassiopi, and Agios Stefanos.

Jet Skiing

Jet skiing is a popular and exciting water sport in Corfu. Several water sports centers on the island offer jet ski rentals and guided tours. The most popular jet skiing spots in Corfu are Kontokali Bay, Dassia Beach, and Gouvia Bay. These beaches offer clear and calm waters, ideal for jet skiing enthusiasts of all levels. If you're new to jet skiing, it's recommended to take a few lessons with a certified instructor to learn the basics and ensure your safety.

Overall, Corfu offers a wide range of water sports activities for all levels of experience. Whether you're looking for a relaxing paddleboarding session or an adrenaline-pumping jet ski ride, there's something for everyone. Just be sure to follow safety guidelines and regulations, and respect the marine life and environment while enjoying these activities.

Hiking

Corfu is a hiker's paradise, with its diverse landscapes and beautiful scenery. Hiking is one of the best ways to explore the island's natural beauty and hidden gems. Here are some more details about the different hiking trails on the island:

The Corfu Trail

The Corfu Trail is a long-distance hiking trail that takes you through some of the most beautiful and varied landscapes on the island. The trail is well-marked with red and white signs, and there are plenty of accommodation options along the way, including guesthouses, tavernas, and campsites.

The trail starts in the south of the island, near the village of Kavos, and follows the west coast northwards, passing through villages such as Agios Gordios, Liapades, and Paleokastritsa. From there, it heads inland through the mountains, passing through the village of Lakones and the historic Angelokastro fortress, before descending to the northern coast and the village of Sidari.

The entire trail can take around 10-12 days to complete, but there are also shorter sections that you can hike in a day or two. Some of the most popular sections include:

- The Paleokastritsa to Lakones section, which passes through stunning coastal scenery and the historic monastery of Paleokastritsa.

- The Liapades to Angelokastro section, which takes you through traditional villages and offers panoramic views of the sea and coastline.

- The Agios Georgios to Arillas section, which passes through beautiful beaches and offers stunning sunset views.

The Pantokrator Trail
The Pantokrator Trail is a challenging but rewarding hike that takes you to the highest point on the island, Mount Pantokrator. The trail starts from the abandoned village of Old Perithia, which is worth exploring in its own right, with its stone houses and narrow alleys.

The trail is approximately 7 kilometers long and takes around 3-4 hours to complete. It can be quite steep in places, but the climb is well worth it for the panoramic views from the summit. On a clear day, you can see as far as Albania and the other Ionian Islands.

The trail passes through dense forests of oak and pine, and you'll also come across the ruins of an old monastery and a Venetian fort along the way.

The Agii Deka Trail

The Agii Deka Trail is a moderate hiking trail that takes you to the summit of the Agii Deka mountain. The trail starts from the village of Benitses and is approximately 5 kilometers long, taking around 2-3 hours to complete.

The trail passes through olive groves and offers panoramic views of the surrounding mountains and coastline. The summit of Agii Deka is also home to an ancient temple dedicated to the gods Apollo and Artemis, which is worth visiting.

Other Hiking Trails

In addition to the Corfu Trail, Pantokrator Trail, and Agii Deka Trail, there are many other hiking trails on the island that offer different levels of difficulty and stunning views.

The Erimitis Trail is a coastal trail that starts from the village of Avlaki and offers stunning views of the sea and nearby islands. The trail is approximately 7 kilometers long and takes around 3 hours to complete.

The Trail of the Gods starts from the village of Paleokastritsa and passes through ancient ruins and historic landmarks. The trail is approximately 8 kilometers long and takes around 3-4 hours to complete.

The Trail of the Achilleion Palace starts from the village of Gastouri and offers views of the palace and its beautiful gardens. The trail is approximately 5 kilometers long and takes around 2-3 hours to complete.

Overall, hiking is a fantastic way to explore Corfu's beautiful landscapes and immerse yourself in the island's natural beauty. With a variety of hiking trails to choose from, there is something for everyone, whether you're an experienced hiker or just looking for a leisurely stroll.

Before setting out on any hike, it's important to be prepared and make sure you have the right gear. Wear sturdy hiking boots or shoes, bring plenty of water and snacks, and make sure you have a map or GPS device to help navigate the trails.

It's also important to be aware of the weather conditions, as some trails can be slippery or dangerous during rainy or windy weather. If in doubt, check with local hiking guides or visitor centers for advice and recommendations.

In addition to hiking, there are many other outdoor activities to enjoy in Corfu, including:

Cycling

Cycling is a great way to explore Corfu's scenic landscapes and villages. There are many cycling routes to choose from, including quiet country roads and coastal paths.

You can rent bikes from local shops and tour companies, or bring your own if you prefer. Many hotels also offer bike rental services or can arrange guided tours.

Some popular cycling routes include the west coast road from Paleokastritsa to Agios Georgios, which offers stunning coastal views, and the route from Kassiopi to Acharavi, which takes you through traditional villages and olive groves.

Horseback Riding

Horseback riding is a unique and memorable way to explore the beautiful landscapes of Corfu. It allows you to enjoy the natural beauty of the island at a relaxed pace, while also getting a taste of local culture and traditions. Here is some more information about horseback riding in Corfu:

There are several stables located throughout the island that offer horseback riding tours for travelers of all levels of experience. Many of these stables are situated in rural areas and offer scenic rides through olive groves, vineyards, and traditional villages.

One of the most popular horseback riding destinations in Corfu is the Achilleion Palace. This beautiful palace, which was once the summer residence of Empress Elizabeth of Austria, is located on the outskirts of Corfu town and offers breathtaking views of the surrounding countryside. Many horseback riding tours include a visit to the palace, allowing you to combine history and culture with your riding experience.

Another popular horseback riding destination in Corfu is the Erimitis Bay, located on the northwest coast of the island. This secluded and picturesque bay can only be reached by foot or by horseback, making it a unique and exclusive destination. The ride to Erimitis Bay takes you through lush greenery and offers stunning views of the Ionian Sea.

If you're an experienced rider, you may want to consider taking a longer ride through the island's countryside. Some stables offer multi-day tours that take you off the beaten path and allow you to explore some of Corfu's hidden gems. These tours typically include accommodations in traditional villages or guesthouses, giving you an opportunity to experience local hospitality and cuisine.

Whether you're a seasoned rider or a beginner, safety is always a top priority. The stables in Corfu provide well-trained horses and experienced guides to ensure your safety and enjoyment during your ride. Helmets are usually provided, and it's recommended that you wear long pants and closed-toe shoes for your comfort and safety.

Overall, horseback riding is a fantastic way to experience the beauty of Corfu and its countryside. With its picturesque landscapes and variety of riding destinations, Corfu offers a unique and memorable riding experience for travelers of all levels of experience.

In conclusion, Corfu offers a variety of outdoor activities for travelers who love to explore and experience nature. Whether you prefer water sports, hiking, or horseback riding, you will find something to suit your interests on this beautiful Greek island.

CHAPTER FIVE

DAY TRIPS FROM CORFU

One of the great advantages of visiting Corfu is its strategic location, allowing you to easily explore nearby islands, historic sites, and natural wonders. Here are some fantastic day trip options from Corfu:

Albania - Butrint National Park and Gjirokaster

Embarking on a day trip from Corfu to Albania allows you to delve into the rich history and stunning landscapes of this neighboring country. Your journey begins with a scenic boat ride from Corfu to the port of Saranda, located on the Albanian Riviera. From there, you'll venture to two remarkable destinations: Butrint National Park and Gjirokaster.

Butrint National Park, a UNESCO World Heritage site, is a mesmerizing archaeological site that dates back to ancient times. As you explore the ruins, you'll uncover layers of history spanning over 2,500 years. The site's strategic location on a hill overlooking a lagoon offers not only historical significance but also breathtaking natural beauty. Walk amidst the remains of the ancient theater, the Roman baths, the Venetian tower, and the Byzantine basilica. Admire the intricate mosaics that have been remarkably preserved, depicting scenes from mythology and daily life. The acropolis, situated on top of the hill, provides panoramic views of the surrounding landscape, including the vivid greenery and the serene waters of Lake Butrint.

After immersing yourself in the ancient wonders of Butrint, you'll continue your journey to the captivating town of Gjirokaster. Known as the "City of Stone," Gjirokaster is a UNESCO-listed town renowned for its well-preserved Ottoman-era architecture and captivating atmosphere. The town's distinct feature is its collection of traditional stone houses, with their unique wooden balconies and narrow cobblestone streets. Begin your exploration by visiting Gjirokaster Castle, a massive fortress that dominates the hilltop. Inside the castle, you'll find the fascinating Gjirokaster National Museum, which showcases artifacts and exhibits that highlight the town's history and culture.

As you wander through the town, be sure to visit the beautifully restored Ottoman-era bazaar, where you can browse local handicrafts, jewelry, and traditional Albanian souvenirs. Take a leisurely stroll through the historic neighborhoods, observing the unique architectural details and enjoying the views of the valley below.

To delve deeper into Gjirokaster's past, visit the Ethnographic Museum, housed in an 18th-century Ottoman-style house. This museum provides a glimpse into the daily lives of the town's residents through its collection of furniture, clothing, and household items.

In Gjirokaster, you'll also have the opportunity to savor traditional Albanian cuisine. Indulge in local specialties such as Byrek (savory pastry filled with cheese or spinach), Tave Kosi (baked lamb and yogurt casserole), and Baklava (sweet pastry with nuts and honey syrup). Don't forget to accompany your meal with a glass of Raki, a popular Albanian spirit.

As your day trip comes to an end, you'll board the boat back to Corfu, carrying with you cherished memories of exploring the historical wonders of Butrint and immersing yourself in the cultural tapestry of Gjirokaster.

Ioannina and Vikos Gorge

Ioannina, a vibrant city situated on the shores of Lake Pamvotis, offers a fascinating blend of history, culture, and natural beauty. Begin your exploration by visiting the old town, known as Kastro. Stroll through its narrow streets lined with traditional houses, browse through charming shops selling local crafts and souvenirs, and stop by one of the cozy cafes to enjoy a cup of Greek coffee. Don't miss the opportunity to visit the Ioannina Castle, which houses the Byzantine Museum. The museum displays a remarkable collection of religious artifacts, icons, and sculptures, offering insight into the rich Byzantine history of the region.

As you wander around Ioannina, take some time to visit the island of Nisi located in Lake Pamvotis. Hop on a boat and cruise across the calm waters to reach the island. Explore the peaceful monasteries, including the famous Monastery of Agios Panteleimon, and enjoy the tranquil atmosphere that pervades the island.

After immersing yourself in the cultural heritage of Ioannina, it's time to venture into the nearby natural wonder, the Vikos Gorge. Considered one of the deepest gorges in the world, Vikos Gorge offers breathtaking vistas and thrilling hiking opportunities. The gorge is part of the Vikos-Aoos National Park, a protected area characterized by its rugged terrain, dense forests, and crystal-clear rivers.

Start your adventure by driving to the village of Monodendri, the gateway to the gorge. From here, you can embark on a trek along well-marked trails that wind through the dramatic landscape. As you hike, be prepared to be amazed by the towering cliffs, lush vegetation, and the sound of the Vikos River rushing below. The most popular hike is the Vikos Gorge trail, which takes you along the edge of the gorge, offering spectacular views. The trail can be challenging, so make sure to wear appropriate hiking gear and carry plenty of water and snacks.

Along the way, you'll have the opportunity to encounter unique flora and fauna, including rare species of birds and wildflowers. Take your time to appreciate the natural beauty and tranquility of this awe-inspiring gorge. If you're an experienced hiker, you can also consider extending your trek to reach the Voidomatis River, where you can cool off with a refreshing swim in its crystal-clear waters.

After a rewarding day of hiking in Vikos Gorge, make your way back to Ioannina and indulge in the local cuisine. Ioannina is famous for its delicious traditional dishes, such as bourdeto (spicy fish stew), kourkoubinia (fried pies), and baklava (sweet pastry). Visit one of the local tavernas and savor the flavors of Epirus while reminiscing about the breathtaking landscapes and cultural experiences of the day.

Whether you're exploring the historical treasures of Ioannina or immersing yourself in the natural wonders of Vikos Gorge, a day trip to this region promises a captivating journey filled with history, culture, and natural splendor.

Corfu's Northwest Coastline

Corfu's northwest coastline is a breathtaking region that showcases the island's natural beauty and offers a mix of stunning beaches, charming villages, and historical landmarks. Let's delve into the details of this captivating area:

Begin your day trip in Paleokastritsa, a picturesque village known for its postcard-perfect setting. Surrounded by verdant hills and azure waters, Paleokastritsa boasts several enchanting beaches to explore. Start by visiting Agios Spyridon Beach, where you can relax on the golden sands and take a refreshing dip in the crystal-clear waters. For a more secluded experience, venture to Alipa Beach, tucked away in a small cove with tranquil turquoise waters perfect for swimming and snorkeling.

To truly appreciate the coastal splendor, embark on a boat tour from Paleokastritsa to discover the hidden gems of the region. Cruise along the coastline, marvel at the impressive rock formations, and enter the mesmerizing sea caves that dot the shoreline. The highlight of the tour is the Blue Eye

Cave, an ethereal cavern where sunlight filters through an underwater opening, creating a mesmerizing blue glow.

After enjoying the coastal delights, make your way to the charming village of Lakones. Perched on a hillside, Lakones offers panoramic vistas of Paleokastritsa's scenic beauty and the azure Ionian Sea. Take a leisurely stroll through the narrow streets, lined with traditional houses adorned with colorful flowers. Browse the local shops for souvenirs and handicrafts, and visit the village square to sample delicious Greek cuisine at one of the traditional tavernas. Don't miss the opportunity to try local specialties such as moussaka, souvlaki, and freshly caught seafood.

Continuing your journey, head to the Angelokastro Fortress, an imposing medieval stronghold perched atop a steep cliff. Built during the Byzantine era, the fortress offers commanding views of the surrounding area, making it an ideal spot for panoramic photography. As you explore the ruins, envision the historical significance of this strategic fortification, which played a crucial role in defending the island against invaders throughout the centuries.

In addition to these main attractions, the northwest coastline of Corfu is dotted with charming beaches and quaint villages waiting to be discovered.

Explore the pebble beach of Agios Georgios Pagon, where you can unwind in a serene setting surrounded by lush greenery. Visit the traditional village of Krini, characterized by its stone houses and narrow alleys, and indulge in local delicacies at the traditional tavernas.

Overall, Corfu's northwest coastline offers a harmonious blend of natural wonders and cultural treasures. From the stunning beaches of Paleokastritsa to the breathtaking views of Lakones and the historical significance of Angelokastro Fortress, this day trip is sure to leave you with lasting memories of Corfu's coastal splendor.

Paxos and Antipaxos Islands

Paxos and Antipaxos are two idyllic islands located just a short boat ride away from Corfu. These hidden gems offer a peaceful retreat and a chance to immerse yourself in the natural beauty of the Ionian Sea.

Paxos, the larger of the two islands, is known for its unspoiled landscapes, charming villages, and serene atmosphere. Start your day trip by taking a ferry or speedboat from Corfu to Gaios, the main port of Paxos. As you arrive, you'll be greeted by the picturesque harbor lined with colorful fishing boats and waterfront cafes. Take a leisurely stroll through the narrow streets of Gaios, adorned with traditional stone houses and vibrant flowers.

Exploring further, visit the village of Lakka, nestled in a natural harbor surrounded by olive groves. Lakka offers a tranquil ambiance and stunning views of the turquoise waters. Relax on one of the nearby beaches or enjoy a meal at a local taverna, savoring the fresh seafood and traditional Greek dishes.

Another charming village worth visiting is Loggos, located on the northeast coast of Paxos. Wander along the waterfront promenade, lined with tavernas and cafes, and explore the tiny alleys adorned with bougainvillea. Don't miss the chance to taste local delicacies, such as the famous Paxos olive oil, and indulge in a refreshing swim at the nearby beaches of Levrechio and Kipiadi.

One of the highlights of a day trip to Paxos is taking a boat excursion to Antipaxos, a small island known for its breathtaking beaches and crystal-clear waters. As you step onto the pristine shores of Antipaxos, you'll feel like you've discovered a true paradise. Voutoumi and Vrika are the most famous beaches on the island, with their white powdery sand and vibrant turquoise waters. Spend the day swimming, snorkeling, or simply basking in the sun's warm embrace.

To truly appreciate the beauty of Antipaxos, consider taking a boat tour that explores the coastline and the sea caves. Marvel at the dramatic cliffs, hidden coves, and the mesmerizing colors of the sea. The boat tours also provide opportunities for diving into the crystal-clear waters and discovering the underwater world teeming with marine life.

If you choose to explore the charming villages and hidden beaches of Paxos or venture to the pristine shores of Antipaxos, a day trip to these islands promises a serene and unforgettable experience. Immerse yourself in the tranquil ambiance, savor the delicious local cuisine, and let the beauty of these islands captivate your senses.

Sivota and Parga

Sivota, also known as Mourtos, is a picturesque coastal town located on the mainland just a short boat trip away from Corfu. Surrounded by lush green hills and turquoise waters, Sivota offers a peaceful and scenic setting for a day trip. As you arrive in the charming natural harbor, you'll be greeted by a cluster of colorful fishing boats bobbing in the water. Take a leisurely stroll along the waterfront promenade, lined with cafes, tavernas, and shops. Relax in one of the seaside cafes and savor the flavors of freshly caught seafood, traditional Greek dishes, and local delicacies. Sivota is renowned for its excellent fish tavernas, where you can enjoy a meal with a view of the sparkling sea.

One of the highlights of Sivota is its stunning beaches. Bella Vraka is a unique beach located on a small island that can be reached by walking through shallow waters. This natural phenomenon creates a lagoon-like setting, perfect for swimming and sunbathing. Mega Ammos is another popular beach known for its crystal-clear waters and soft golden sand. Spend some time unwinding on the beach, soaking up the sun, and taking refreshing dips in the refreshing sea.

For those interested in maritime adventures, Sivota offers opportunities for boat trips and excursions. You can hire a small boat or join a guided tour to explore the nearby secluded coves, hidden beaches, and picturesque islets. Discover secret caves, snorkel in the clear waters, and admire the untouched beauty of the Ionian Sea.

Parga

Continuing the day trip from Sivota, head to the enchanting town of Parga. Situated on the mainland, Parga is a postcard-perfect destination with its colorful houses, cobblestone streets, and cascading bougainvillea. As you approach the town, you'll be captivated by the panoramic views of Parga's Venetian Castle perched on a hilltop. The castle, built in the 14th century, is a prominent landmark and offers a glimpse into the town's rich history.

Wander through the narrow streets of the old town, filled with boutique shops, charming cafes, and traditional tavernas. Explore the lively central square, where you can relax under the shade of trees and people-watch while enjoying a coffee or a refreshing drink. Take time to visit the Church of Panagia, an iconic white-washed church that stands proudly at the center of the town. Inside, you'll find beautiful religious icons and intricate artwork.

For panoramic views of Parga and its surrounding beauty, climb up to the Venetian Castle. The castle ruins provide a mesmerizing backdrop, and from the top, you'll be rewarded with breathtaking vistas of the town, the Ionian Sea, and the nearby islands. Capture the moment with stunning photographs and immerse yourself in the tranquil atmosphere.

Parga boasts several stunning beaches where you can relax and swim. Valtos Beach, located just a short distance from the town, is a popular choice. It offers a long stretch of golden sand, clear waters, and a variety of beach bars and tavernas. Spend your afternoon basking in the sun, taking refreshing dips in the sea, and indulging in beachside snacks and drinks.

As the day winds down, Parga comes alive with a vibrant nightlife. The town offers a variety of bars, clubs, and live music venues, creating a buzzing atmosphere. Enjoy a cocktail at a waterfront bar or dance the night away to lively Greek music.

Returning to Corfu after a day exploring Sivota and Parga, you'll have experienced the natural beauty, historic landmarks, and cultural traditions of the Ionian region. Whether you choose to embark on a boat trip, relax on the beach, or wander through charming towns, a day trip from Corfu to Sivota and Parga is a memorable experience that will leave you enchanted with the beauty and charm of Greece.

Achilleion Palace and Kanoni

Located in the village of Gastouri, just a short distance from Corfu Town, Achilleion Palace is a true gem that combines architectural splendor with rich history. Built in the late 19th century, the palace was commissioned by Empress Elisabeth of Austria, also known as Sisi. Inspired by Greek mythology and the tragic hero Achilles, the palace showcases a fusion of neoclassical and Pompeian styles.

Upon entering the palace, visitors are greeted by the grandeur of the main hall, adorned with magnificent frescoes and statues. Explore the various rooms, each exquisitely decorated and showcasing a unique theme. Marvel at the stunning artworks, luxurious furnishings, and intricate details that reflect the opulence of the era.

The highlight of the palace is undoubtedly the famous statue of Achilles, located in the palace gardens. Standing at the center of a beautiful terrace, the statue depicts Achilles in all his glory, poised for battle. The terrace offers panoramic views of the surrounding landscape, including the Ionian Sea and the lush greenery of Corfu.

Take your time to wander through the palace gardens, meticulously landscaped with lush vegetation, colorful flowers, and charming pathways. The serene atmosphere and breathtaking views create a tranquil oasis, perfect for relaxation and contemplation.

Achilleion Palace has also served as a historical backdrop, hosting important events and gatherings throughout the years. It has attracted notable figures, including European royalty and renowned personalities of the time.

Kanoni

Located on the outskirts of Corfu Town, the Kanoni area offers a picturesque setting with panoramic views and cultural significance. The name "Kanoni" derives from the cannons (kanonades) that were once positioned here to defend the island against invasions.

The main attraction of Kanoni is the iconic view of Mouse Island (Pontikonisi). This small islet, adorned with a charming Byzantine church, is one of the most recognizable landmarks of Corfu. Legend has it that Mouse Island is the petrified ship of Odysseus, turned to stone by the god Poseidon. Enjoy the view from the Kanoni viewpoint, where you can see the islet surrounded by turquoise waters.

Adjacent to Kanoni is the Vlacherna Monastery, a quaint monastery connected to the mainland by a small causeway. Explore the monastery's peaceful courtyard, adorned with colorful flowers and shaded by cypress trees. From here, you can also take a boat ride to visit Mouse Island and experience its tranquil ambiance up close.

Kanoni is also known for its vibrant waterfront cafes, where you can relax with a refreshing beverage or savor traditional Greek cuisine while enjoying the breathtaking views. As the sun sets, the area transforms into a magical setting, with the illuminated Mouse Island and the glittering lights of Corfu Town creating a romantic ambiance.

It doesn't matter if you visit Achilleion Palace to delve into the grandeur of the past or explore the panoramic beauty of Kanoni, both destinations offer unique experiences that showcase the charm and allure of Corfu.

In conclusion, Corfu's strategic location provides ample opportunities for day trips to explore nearby islands, historical sites, and natural wonders. From the idyllic islands of Paxos and Antipaxos to the ancient ruins of Butrint National Park in Albania, there is something to suit every traveler's interests. Whether you prefer to immerse yourself in history, bask in the beauty of nature, or enjoy thrilling water activities, the day trip options from Corfu offer a diverse range of experiences. Take advantage of the island's accessibility and embark on unforgettable journeys that will enhance your Corfu vacation.

CHAPTER SIX

FOOD AND DRINK IN CORFU

Corfu's cuisine is a unique blend of Greek, Italian, and British influences, reflecting the island's history as a crossroads of different cultures. The island is known for its use of fresh, local ingredients, including seafood, olives, and herbs.

Traditional Dishes

Corfu's traditional dishes showcase the island's rich culinary heritage, blending Greek, Italian, and British flavors to create a unique gastronomic experience. Here are some more details about the traditional dishes you can savor in Corfu:

Pastitsada: Pastitsada is a beloved Corfiot dish that exemplifies the island's fusion of culinary influences. It consists of slow-cooked beef, typically braised in a flavorful tomato sauce infused with spices like cinnamon, cloves, and allspice. The tender beef is served with thick, hollow pasta called macaroni, which absorbs the delicious sauce, resulting in a hearty and comforting dish.

Sofrito: Another iconic dish of Corfu is sofrito, featuring thin slices of veal simmered in a fragrant sauce made with white wine, garlic, vinegar, and sometimes a touch of cinnamon. The meat is cooked until it becomes tender and flavorful, often accompanied by a side of creamy mashed potatoes or fluffy rice. The delicate balance of flavors and the tenderness of the veal make sofrito a true culinary delight.

Bourdeto: Seafood lovers should not miss the opportunity to try bourdeto, a spicy fish stew that exemplifies Corfu's coastal cuisine. Typically made with local fish like scorpionfish or cod, the dish is cooked with a spicy tomato-based sauce, garlic, red chili peppers, and a hint of vinegar. The result is a tantalizing blend of flavors that showcases the island's bold and vibrant culinary traditions.

Savoro: Savoro is a delightful fish dish that showcases Corfu's culinary ties to Venetian cuisine. Whole fish, often small local species like whitebait or smelt, are marinated in a tangy mixture of vinegar, garlic, and herbs. The fish is then lightly fried and served with caramelized onions, raisins, and pine nuts, creating a harmonious balance of sweet and savory flavors.

Vegetarian Delights: Corfu also caters to vegetarian palates with delicious traditional dishes. Spanakorizo is a simple yet satisfying dish made with tender spinach and fragrant rice cooked in a flavorful broth. Gigantes plaki features giant beans cooked in a tomato-based sauce with aromatic herbs, creating a hearty and nutritious vegetarian option.

Kumquat Delicacies: Kumquat, a small citrus fruit native to Corfu, plays a prominent role in the island's cuisine. Apart from being used to make liqueur and wine, kumquat is also incorporated into various desserts and sweets. Kumquat preserves, marmalades, and candies offer a delightful balance of sweet and tangy flavors, making them perfect accompaniments to local pastries and desserts.

Pastitsio: Although pastitsada is a popular dish in Corfu, it's worth mentioning another Greek classic that has found its way to the island's culinary scene: pastitsio. This baked pasta dish consists of layers of macaroni pasta, seasoned ground meat (often a combination of beef and pork), and a creamy béchamel sauce. The dish is then baked to golden perfection, resulting in a comforting and flavorful delight.

Sofrito di Maiale: In addition to the veal sofrito, Corfu is also known for its variation of sofrito made with pork. Sofrito di Maiale features thin slices of pork simmered in a similar sauce as the veal sofrito, combining white wine, garlic, vinegar, and fragrant spices. The result is tender and succulent pork with a delightful medley of flavors.

Pasteli: Pasteli is a traditional sweet treat that has been enjoyed in Corfu for generations. This delectable confection consists of sesame seeds bound together with honey or grape syrup. The mixture is cooked until it forms a chewy texture and then cut into small bars or bites. Pasteli is not only a delightful snack but also a beloved symbol of Corfu's culinary heritage.

Mandolato: Mandolato is a traditional Corfiot nougat made from a blend of almonds, honey, and sugar. This sweet delicacy has a soft, chewy texture and is often studded with dried fruits like raisins or chopped figs. Mandolato is particularly popular during festivals and holidays, making it a delightful gift or souvenir to bring back home.

Ladotyri: Ladotyri is a unique and flavorful cheese that is produced exclusively on the island of Corfu. This traditional cheese is made from sheep or goat milk and is aged in olive oil, infusing it with a distinctive and rich flavor. Ladotyri has a firm texture and a tangy, salty taste, making it a delightful addition to cheese platters or enjoyed on its own.

Bourekia: Bourekia are savory pastries that have their roots in the Ottoman cuisine but have become a beloved local treat in Corfu. These small, bite-sized pastries are filled with a variety of ingredients, such as cheese, spinach, or minced meat. They are typically baked until golden and crispy, offering a satisfying snack or appetizer option.

Local Ingredients

Corfu is blessed with an abundance of local ingredients that contribute to the island's vibrant and flavorful cuisine. From the renowned olive oil to unique fruits and cheeses, here are some more details about the local ingredients that add a distinctive touch to Corfu's gastronomy:

Olive Oil: Corfu's olive oil is renowned for its exceptional quality and flavor. The island's fertile soil, ideal climate, and traditional cultivation methods result in olives that produce a rich and fruity oil. The locals take pride in their olive oil production, which is often cold-pressed to preserve its nutrients and distinct taste. You can visit olive groves and mills, such as the Governor's Olive Mill in Liapades, to witness the olive oil production process and sample the different varieties.

Kumquats: Corfu is famous for its cultivation of kumquats, small citrus fruits that are a true delight for the senses. The island's microclimate provides the perfect conditions for kumquat trees to thrive.

These tangy and aromatic fruits are often enjoyed fresh, but they are also utilized in various culinary creations. Kumquats are transformed into delicious marmalades, syrups, liqueurs, and candies. You can explore the Kumquat Distillery in the village of Benitses, where you can learn about the fruit's history and production while tasting its delightful products.

Local Cheeses: Cheese lovers will be in heaven when exploring the local cheese offerings in Corfu. The island produces a variety of artisanal cheeses, each with its own unique characteristics. Here are a few notable examples:

Feta: A classic Greek cheese, feta is made from sheep's or goat's milk. It is creamy, tangy, and crumbly, often used as a topping for salads, pastries, or enjoyed simply with olives and bread.

Ladotiri: Ladotiri is a traditional Corfiot cheese made from sheep's or goat's milk. It has a slightly sweet and rich flavor and is aged in olive oil-soaked cloth, which imparts a distinctive aroma. It can be enjoyed on its own or grated over pasta dishes.

Anthotyro: This soft, fresh cheese is made from a mixture of sheep's and goat's milk. It has a mild, slightly sweet taste and a creamy texture. Anthotyro is often used in salads or as a filling for pastries and pies.

San Michali: San Michali is a semi-hard cheese with a nutty and buttery flavor. It is made from sheep's milk and is aged for several months, developing a firm texture and complex taste. This cheese is best enjoyed on a cheese board or paired with local honey and nuts.

Honey: Another outstanding local ingredient in Corfu is honey. The island's diverse flora, including wildflowers, aromatic herbs, and citrus blossoms, contribute to the unique flavors and aromas found in Corfiot honey. Beekeeping is a longstanding tradition on the island, and you can find a wide variety of honey types, such as thyme, pine, and wildflower honey. Visit local markets or specialized honey shops to explore the different varieties and indulge in the natural sweetness of Corfu's honey.

Herbs and Spices: Corfu is home to a plethora of aromatic herbs and spices that add depth and complexity to its traditional dishes. Oregano, thyme, rosemary, and bay leaves are commonly used in cooking, infusing dishes with their distinctive aromas.

These herbs are often handpicked from the mountains and countryside, ensuring their freshness and potency. Additionally, spices like cinnamon, allspice, and cloves are frequently employed in recipes, especially in savory dishes like pastitsada and bourdeto. Exploring local markets and specialty stores allows you to purchase these fragrant herbs and spices to enhance your own culinary creations or bring a touch of Corfu's flavors back home.

Seafood: As an island, Corfu boasts an abundance of fresh and succulent seafood. From sardines and anchovies to octopus and sea bream, the local seafood is celebrated for its quality and taste. Fishermen bring in their catches daily, ensuring that restaurants and tavernas serve dishes made with the freshest ingredients. Grilled, fried, or marinated in olive oil and lemon, Corfu's seafood dishes highlight the island's coastal charm and provide a true taste of the Mediterranean.

While exploring the culinary landscape of Corfu, consider joining guided tours or cooking classes that provide insight into the island's traditional ingredients and cooking techniques. These experiences allow you to immerse yourself in the local culture, interact with passionate food experts, and create your own Corfiot-inspired dishes.

Exploring the traditional dishes of Corfu is a culinary adventure that allows travelers to delve into the island's history, cultural influences, and unique flavors. Whether you're a fan of meat, seafood, or vegetarian fare, Corfu's gastronomy offers a wide range of options to satisfy every palate. From hearty stews to sweet indulgences, the traditional dishes of Corfu are sure to leave a lasting impression on your taste buds.

Local Wines and drinks

Corfu's wine production is one of the island's most treasured traditions, with a history dating back to ancient times. The island's terroir, with its fertile soil, mild climate, and proximity to the sea, provides ideal conditions for growing grapes that produce wines with unique aromas and flavors.

Corfu boasts a diverse range of indigenous grape varieties that contribute to the island's unique winemaking tradition. These local grape varieties thrive in the island's specific climate, soil conditions, and winemaking techniques, resulting in wines with distinctive characteristics.

Kakotrygis: Kakotrygis is a white grape variety that is native to Corfu and is primarily cultivated on the island. It produces wines with a pale yellow color and a delicate aroma. Kakotrygis wines are known for their vibrant acidity, citrusy notes, and hints of tropical fruits, making them a refreshing choice for warm summer days.

Petrokoritho: Petrokoritho is another white grape variety indigenous to Corfu. It is highly prized for its ability to produce wines with excellent structure and complexity. Petrokoritho wines often display a beautiful golden hue, a rich mouthfeel, and a bouquet of ripe fruits, including peach, pear, and apricot. They pair well with seafood, poultry, and creamy cheeses.

Robola: Robola is perhaps the most celebrated grape variety of Corfu. It is primarily grown in the Paliki region of the island, where the vineyards benefit from the limestone-rich soil and cool mountain breezes. Robola wines are characterized by their vibrant acidity, citrusy aromas, and mineral undertones. They often exhibit a pale yellow color, and on the palate, they offer a balance of crispness and richness. Robola pairs excellently with seafood, salads, and light pasta dishes.

Skopelitiko: Skopelitiko is a red grape variety native to Corfu, primarily grown in the northern part of the island. The wines produced from Skopelitiko grapes are typically medium-bodied with a deep ruby color. They showcase aromas of red berries, spices, and a touch of earthiness. On the palate, Skopelitiko wines display soft tannins, good acidity, and a lingering finish. They pair well with grilled meats, roasted vegetables, and aged cheeses.

These local grape varieties contribute to the rich tapestry of wines found in Corfu. They reflect the island's terroir, cultural heritage, and the skill of the winemakers who carefully nurture the vines and craft the wines. Exploring the different expressions of these local varieties is an excellent way to appreciate the unique flavors and character of Corfu's wines.

Tsitsibira: In addition to wine, Corfu is also known for its traditional beverage called Tsitsibira. Tsitsibira is a non-alcoholic, lightly carbonated drink made from fermented barley and flavored with various herbs, such as rosemary and mint. It has a unique and refreshing taste, reminiscent of a mild herbal soda. Tsitsibira is a popular choice for those looking for a non-alcoholic beverage option to accompany their meals or for a refreshing sip on a hot day.

Kumquat Liqueur: While not a wine, Kumquat liqueur is a local specialty that deserves a mention. Kumquats, small citrus fruits grown abundantly in Corfu, are used to produce a delightful liqueur. The liqueur has a sweet and tangy flavor, capturing the essence of the vibrant fruit. It can be enjoyed as an aperitif or digestif and is also used in cocktails and desserts. Sampling Kumquat liqueur is a must for those looking to experience the unique flavors of Corfu

White Wines:
Corfu's white wines are celebrated for their freshness, vibrant flavors, and ability to capture the essence of the island's terroir.

Moschato: Moschato, also known as Moscato or Muscat, is a sweet white wine produced in Corfu. It is made from the Muscat Blanc grape variety, which thrives in the island's warm climate. Moschato wine boasts a bright golden color and exudes an enticing floral aroma reminiscent of jasmine, orange blossoms, and rose petals. Its taste profile is rich and luscious, with flavors of ripe peaches, apricots, and honey. Moschato is often enjoyed as a dessert wine, paired with sweet treats like baklava, fruit tarts, or soft cheeses. It can also be savored on its own as a delightful aperitif.

Other White Varieties

In addition to Robola and Moschato, Corfu's winemakers cultivate other white grape varieties that contribute to the island's diverse wine selection. These include Kakotrygis, Petrokoritho, and Skopelitiko. While less commonly known outside the region, these varieties produce intriguing and unique wines that offer a different tasting experience. Winemakers experiment with these indigenous grapes, crafting white wines with their distinct characteristics, ranging from aromatic and fruity to more floral and complex profiles.

Wine Tourism: Corfu has embraced wine tourism, offering visitors the opportunity to explore vineyards, wineries, and tasting rooms. Several wineries welcome guests for tours, where they can learn about the winemaking process, walk through vineyards, and enjoy guided tastings of the island's finest wines. These wine tours provide a deeper understanding of Corfu's winemaking traditions and allow visitors to appreciate the passion and dedication of the local producers.

Whether you prefer dry, crisp whites or sweet, aromatic delights, Corfu's white wines offer a delightful range of options to please every wine lover's palate. So, raise a glass and savor the flavors of Corfu's remarkable white wines, toasting to the island's rich viticultural heritage.

Overall, Corfu's local wines and drinks offer a glimpse into the island's rich cultural heritage and unique terroir. Whether it's savoring the crisp and refreshing white wines made from local grape varieties like Robola, exploring the rich flavors of Skopelitiko red wines, or enjoying traditional beverages like Tsitsibira and Kumquat liqueur, there are plenty of options to satisfy every palate. Embrace the island's gastronomic delights and raise a glass to the flavors of Corfu.

Dining Experiences

Corfu offers a diverse range of dining experiences that cater to all tastes and preferences. From traditional tavernas serving home-style Greek cuisine to upscale restaurants with creative fusion dishes, there is something for everyone. Here are some dining experiences you can enjoy in Corfu:

Tavernas

The quintessential Corfiot dining experience can be found in the charming tavernas scattered throughout the island. These family-run establishments exude warmth and hospitality, providing an authentic taste of Greek cuisine.

Here are some Tavernas popular among locals and visitors alike:

To Steki Tou Thanasi (Corfu Town)

Located in the heart of Corfu Town, To Steki Tou Thanasi is a popular taverna known for its authentic Greek cuisine and welcoming atmosphere. The menu features a wide array of traditional dishes, including moussaka, souvlaki, stuffed vine leaves (dolmades), and freshly caught seafood. The outdoor seating area offers a charming ambiance, allowing diners to enjoy their meal while observing the bustling streets of the Old Town.

Taverna Tripa (Paleokastritsa)

Nestled in the scenic village of Paleokastritsa, Taverna Tripa is a hidden gem overlooking the crystal-clear waters of the Ionian Sea. This family-run taverna serves homemade Corfiot dishes using locally sourced ingredients. From grilled octopus and marinated anchovies to stifado (slow-cooked beef stew) and pastitsio (Greek-style lasagna), the menu showcases the flavors of the region. Diners can relax on the outdoor terrace, enjoying the panoramic views and the gentle sea breeze.

Taverna Agni (Agni Bay)

Agni Bay is renowned for its picturesque beauty, and Taverna Agni complements the stunning surroundings with its exceptional dining experience. This waterfront taverna specializes in fresh seafood delicacies. Guests can savor dishes like grilled sea bream, prawn linguine, and seafood risotto while gazing out at the idyllic bay. The friendly staff and relaxed atmosphere make Taverna Agni a must-visit destination for seafood lovers.

Taverna George & Elena (Sidari)

Situated in the lively resort town of Sidari, Taverna George & Elena is a family-friendly taverna that has been serving delicious Greek cuisine for decades. The extensive menu features classic Greek dishes prepared with care and attention to detail. From Greek salads and souvlaki to lamb chops and spanakopita (spinach pie), there is something to please every palate. The cozy interior and outdoor seating area provide a comfortable setting for enjoying a satisfying meal.

Taverna Agios Stefanos (Agios Stefanos)

Located in the charming village of Agios Stefanos in northwest Corfu, Taverna Agios Stefanos offers a delightful dining experience with traditional Corfiot flavors. The menu showcases local ingredients and features dishes like pastitsada, sofrito, and kleftiko (slow-cooked lamb). With its welcoming atmosphere and beautiful views of the surrounding countryside, this taverna captures the essence of Corfu's culinary heritage.

These tavernas represent just a handful of the many wonderful dining options available throughout Corfu. From the bustling streets of Corfu Town to the tranquil bays and villages, each taverna offers its own unique charm, warm hospitality, and a chance to savor the authentic flavors of the island.

Farm-to-Table Experiences

Corfu's farm-to-table dining experiences offer a unique opportunity to immerse yourself in the island's local produce and sustainable farming practices. These experiences often take place in scenic countryside locations, allowing you to appreciate the beauty of Corfu's rural landscapes while enjoying a farm-fresh meal. Here are a few notable farm-to-table venues and their locations on the island:

Ambelonas: Located in the village of Rachtades, Ambelonas offers a captivating farm-to-table experience. Situated within a vineyard, this establishment showcases organic farming methods and traditional viticulture practices. Explore the vineyards, olive groves, and herb gardens before indulging in a meal that highlights the bounty of their own produce. From freshly picked fruits and vegetables to homemade olive oil and wine, Ambelonas provides an authentic taste of Corfu's agricultural heritage.

Govino Bay Farm-to-Table: Situated near the village of Gouvia, Govino Bay offers a farm-to-table experience within a picturesque setting. The restaurant sources its ingredients directly from its own organic farm, ensuring that every dish is made with the freshest produce. The farm cultivates a wide range of fruits, vegetables, and herbs, allowing guests to savor seasonal flavors in dishes prepared with care and creativity.

Agroktima Agris: Nestled in the village of Sgourades, Agroktima Agris is a charming farm-to-table venue that showcases the island's agricultural traditions. With its own organic farm, the restaurant emphasizes the use of fresh, locally sourced ingredients. Guests can explore the farm, interact with animals, and learn about traditional farming practices. The menu features dishes crafted from the farm's own fruits, vegetables, and meats, offering an authentic taste of Corfu's countryside.

Farm-to-Table Experiences at Olive Oil Producers: Many olive oil producers in Corfu offer farm-to-table experiences as well. These experiences allow visitors to witness the olive oil production process, from the harvest to the pressing, and often include a meal featuring dishes prepared with the farm's own olive oil. As you savor the flavors of the Mediterranean cuisine, you'll gain a deeper understanding of the importance of olive oil in Corfu's culinary traditions.

These farm-to-table venues not only provide exceptional dining experiences but also offer an educational insight into the island's agricultural heritage. They allow visitors to appreciate the connection between the land, the ingredients, and the flavors that make Corfu's cuisine unique.

Fine Dining and Fusion Cuisine

Corfu boasts a selection of upscale restaurants that offer a fine dining experience and showcase the artistry of fusion cuisine. These establishments are often located in picturesque settings, providing a perfect backdrop for a memorable meal. Here are a few locations where you can indulge in fine dining and fusion cuisine in Corfu:

The capital city of Corfu, Corfu Town, is home to several fine dining restaurants that excel in fusion cuisine. Wander through the narrow streets of the UNESCO-listed Old Town and discover hidden gems tucked away in charming squares and alleyways. Many of these restaurants combine traditional Greek flavors with international influences, resulting in innovative and tantalizing dishes. Enjoy a sophisticated dining experience in elegant surroundings, often with outdoor seating that allows you to soak up the ambiance of this historic city.

Corfu's coastal resorts also feature high-end restaurants that specialize in fusion cuisine. Locations such as Glyfada, Dassia, or Kassiopi offer breathtaking sea views and provide an idyllic setting for a luxurious dining experience. These restaurants often have a contemporary and stylish atmosphere, combining modern décor with elements that reflect the island's natural beauty. You can indulge in gourmet creations that blend local ingredients with global culinary influences, resulting in a harmonious fusion of flavors. Immerse yourself in the coastal charm and relish the exquisite dishes crafted by skilled chefs.

Many of Corfu's exclusive resorts and upscale hotels boast their own fine dining establishments. These establishments often prioritize using fresh, local ingredients sourced from the island's bountiful produce. Enjoy panoramic views of the Ionian Sea or beautifully landscaped gardens as you savor meticulously crafted dishes. The chefs in these establishments are known for their culinary expertise, blending international techniques with the island's rich culinary traditions. These venues offer an all-encompassing experience, combining exceptional food, elegant ambiance, and impeccable service

Overall, in these fine dining and fusion cuisine locations, you can expect exquisite presentations, creative flavor combinations, and an extensive selection of wines and spirits to complement your meal. The attention to detail, quality ingredients, and the commitment to culinary excellence make these establishments a must-visit for discerning diners seeking a refined gastronomic experience in Corfu.

Seafront Restaurants
Corfu's stunning coastline and idyllic beaches provide the perfect setting for seafront restaurants that offer not only exceptional cuisine but also breathtaking views of the sea. These establishments allow you to enjoy a memorable dining experience while immersing yourself in the beauty of the island.

Here's what you can expect from seafront restaurants in Corfu:

Location and Ambiance: Seafront restaurants in Corfu are strategically positioned along the coastline, some perched on cliffs overlooking the sea, while others are right on the sandy shores. As you enter these establishments, you are greeted by a serene and inviting ambiance, often adorned with tasteful décor that complements the seaside setting. The gentle sound of waves crashing against the shore and the salty sea breeze create a relaxing atmosphere that enhances your dining experience.

Panoramic Views: One of the highlights of dining at a seafront restaurant is the breathtaking views they offer. From your table, you can take in panoramic vistas of the turquoise waters stretching out to the horizon. The ever-changing colors of the sea, the sunlight dancing on the waves, and the distant islands on the horizon create a mesmerizing backdrop that adds to the enchantment of your meal. Whether you choose to dine during the day, as the sun sparkles on the water, or in the evening, as the sky transforms into a canvas of vibrant hues, the views from these restaurants are truly unforgettable.

Fresh Seafood Delicacies: Seafront restaurants in Corfu are renowned for their emphasis on fresh seafood. The menus boast an array of dishes featuring locally sourced fish and shellfish. Indulge in delicacies such as grilled sea bass or sea bream, succulent prawns, flavorful lobster, or a platter of mixed seafood that brings together the best of the ocean's offerings. The chefs skillfully prepare the seafood, often incorporating local herbs, olive oil, and citrus flavors to enhance the natural taste and freshness of the ingredients. Pair your seafood feast with a crisp white wine or a chilled ouzo for a perfect culinary combination.

Mediterranean and Greek Cuisine: While seafood takes center stage, seafront restaurants in Corfu also offer a variety of Mediterranean and Greek dishes to cater to different preferences. Explore a diverse menu that showcases the island's culinary traditions, featuring dishes like Greek salads bursting with ripe tomatoes, cucumbers, feta cheese, and Kalamata olives, or moussaka, a classic Greek casserole layered with eggplant, minced meat, and creamy béchamel sauce. Vegetarian options, such as stuffed vine leaves (dolmades) and spanakopita (spinach and feta pie), are also available, ensuring that there's something for everyone.

Romantic Dining Experience: With their enchanting settings and breathtaking views, seafront restaurants in Corfu are an ideal choice for a romantic dinner. As the sun sets over the sea, these establishments create an intimate and cozy ambiance, perfect for a romantic evening. Enjoy candlelit dinners under the stars, savoring exquisite dishes while creating lasting memories with your loved one. Whether you're celebrating a special occasion or simply want to spend quality time together, the romantic atmosphere of seafront restaurants in Corfu sets the stage for a truly unforgettable experience.

The combination of picturesque views, fresh seafood delicacies, Mediterranean flavors, and a romantic ambiance make dining at a seafront restaurant in Corfu a highlight of your visit. Immerse yourself in the coastal charm and indulge in an extraordinary culinary journey as you savor the best that the island has to offer.

In conclusion, if you prefer traditional tavernas, seaside dining, farm-to-table experiences, or fine dining fusion cuisine, Corfu has a diverse range of dining options to suit every palate and occasion. Explore the island's culinary landscape and let your taste buds embark on a delightful journey through the flavors of Corfu.

CHAPTER SEVEN

NIGHTLIFE IN CORFU

Corfu is not only renowned for its natural beauty and historical attractions but also for its vibrant and exciting nightlife. The island offers a diverse range of entertainment options, from energetic clubs to laid-back bars, ensuring that there is something for everyone. If you're seeking a wild night out or a more relaxed evening, Corfu has it all.

Bars and Tavernas

Corfu is home to a wide array of bars and tavernas, each offering a unique atmosphere and culinary delights. Whether you're looking for a laid-back evening with traditional Greek music or a trendy cocktail bar serving innovative drinks, Corfu has something to suit every taste. Here are some of the highlights:

Liston Square

Located in the heart of Corfu Town, Liston Square is a vibrant hub of activity and a popular gathering spot for both locals and tourists. The area is lined with charming cafés and bars, offering outdoor seating where you can enjoy a drink while admiring the elegant architecture and watching the world go by. Liston Square is particularly lively in the evenings, with live music often filling the air, creating a delightful ambiance.

Spianada
Adjacent to Liston Square, Spianada is one of the largest public squares in Europe and a prime location for experiencing Corfu's nightlife. Here, you'll find a variety of bars and tavernas catering to different preferences. Some venues offer traditional Greek music, allowing you to immerse yourself in the island's cultural heritage, while others provide a more modern and cosmopolitan atmosphere with DJs and contemporary music.

Old Town Bars
Exploring the narrow streets of Corfu's Old Town reveals hidden gems in the form of cozy bars and tavernas. These establishments often have a rustic charm, with stone walls and traditional décor. Here, you can unwind with a glass of ouzo or try local beers while enjoying live music performances by talented Greek musicians. The intimate setting and warm hospitality create an authentic and memorable experience.

Gouvia Marina
Gouvia Marina, located on the east coast of the island, offers a unique setting for enjoying a drink or

a meal. The marina is surrounded by a selection of stylish bars and waterfront restaurants, providing stunning views of the boats and yachts. Whether you prefer a refreshing cocktail, a glass of local wine, or a delicious seafood dinner, Gouvia Marina is an excellent choice for a sophisticated and relaxing evening.

Paleokastritsa

Paleokastritsa, known for its picturesque bays and crystal-clear waters, is not only a popular daytime destination but also offers an enticing nightlife scene. Along the waterfront, you'll find bars and tavernas with open-air seating, allowing you to savor your drink while enjoying the breathtaking views of the sea. Some establishments organize live music events, creating a lively atmosphere where you can dance and socialize until the late hours.

Traditional Greek Tavernas

Throughout Corfu, you'll come across numerous traditional Greek tavernas that offer an authentic taste of the island's cuisine and culture. These tavernas serve an array of Greek dishes, from moussaka and souvlaki to fresh seafood and local specialties. Enjoy your meal accompanied by traditional Greek music and dance performances, creating an unforgettable dining experience.

When exploring the bars and tavernas of Corfu, take the opportunity to sample the local drinks, such as ouzo, tsipouro, and the refreshing Corfu beer. Don't be afraid to ask the friendly staff for recommendations on the best local specialties and traditional dishes to try. The island's vibrant bar and taverna scene ensures that you'll have a memorable and enjoyable evening out during your stay in Corfu.

Beach Bars

Corfu's beach bars are a major highlight of the island's nightlife, offering visitors a unique and enjoyable experience by combining stunning coastal views, refreshing drinks, and a lively atmosphere. These beachfront establishments are scattered across the island, allowing you to find the perfect spot to relax and soak up the sun during the day and party by the water at night.

Pink Palace Beach Bar (Agios Gordios)

Situated on the golden sands of Agios Gordios Beach, the Pink Palace Beach Bar is a popular hotspot known for its vibrant and energetic ambiance. During the day, you can lounge on sunbeds or take part in water sports activities, while in the evening, the bar transforms into a lively party venue. Dance to the latest tunes, sip on colorful cocktails, and mingle with fellow travelers as the DJ spins infectious beats.

Kavos Beach Bar (Kavos)

Located in the vibrant resort town of Kavos, Kavos Beach Bar is a must-visit destination for those seeking a lively beach party atmosphere. With its prime beachfront location and energetic vibe, this bar is renowned for its wild parties that continue well into the early hours of the morning. Enjoy a variety of music genres, including house, EDM, and hip-hop, while sipping on signature cocktails and taking in the electrifying atmosphere.

Canal d'Amour Beach Bar (Sidari)

Situated on the popular Sidari Beach, Canal d'Amour Beach Bar offers a more laid-back and relaxed setting compared to the high-energy clubs. This beach bar is known for its enchanting views of the unique Canal d'Amour rock formations and the crystal-clear waters. Unwind with a refreshing drink in hand, lounge on sunbeds, and enjoy the serene ambiance as you take in the breathtaking surroundings.

Glyfada Beach Bar (Glyfada)

Nestled along the picturesque Glyfada Beach, Glyfada Beach Bar provides a tranquil setting for a beachside escape. The bar offers a stylish and comfortable atmosphere with chic loungers and umbrellas, allowing you to relax and indulge in the natural beauty of the area. Sip on exotic cocktails, sample delicious snacks, and enjoy the gentle sounds of the waves while basking in the sun or witnessing a stunning sunset.

Pelekas Beach Bar (Pelekas)

Perched on the sandy shores of Pelekas Beach, Pelekas Beach Bar offers a more intimate and romantic atmosphere. This beach bar is known for its idyllic setting, surrounded by lush green hills and crystal-clear waters. Enjoy a quiet evening with your loved one, savoring handcrafted cocktails, and relishing the tranquility of the beach as the sun dips below the horizon.

Many of these beach bars also host special events, including beach parties, live music performances, and themed nights, adding an extra layer of excitement to your beachside experience. Whether you're looking to dance the night away or unwind with a cocktail in hand, Corfu's beach bars offer a diverse range of options to suit your preferences, making them an essential part of the island's vibrant nightlife scene.

Clubs and Nightclubs

Clubs and nightclubs are a major component of Corfu's nightlife, offering visitors an exciting and energetic party scene that keeps going until the early hours of the morning. Corfu's clubs cater to a diverse range of music genres, ensuring that there is something for everyone. The island's most famous clubbing destination is Kavos, located on the southern coast of Corfu, where you can find some of the best clubs and parties on the island.

Kavos is known for its vibrant nightlife scene, attracting young travelers and party enthusiasts from all over the world. The area features a variety of nightclubs that offer a mix of music genres, including electronic, house, hip-hop, and R&B, among others. Clubs such as Future Club and Atlantis Club are among the most popular venues in Kavos, known for their energetic crowds, top-notch DJs, and pulsating music. These clubs feature state-of-the-art sound and lighting systems, ensuring a mesmerizing and unforgettable experience for visitors.

Corfu Town also offers a range of clubbing options, catering to a more diverse crowd. Clubs such as Sinagogi Club and Loft Club are located in the heart of Corfu Town and offer a mix of music genres, including house, techno, and dance. The venues have an electric atmosphere and attract both locals and tourists, providing a unique and immersive clubbing experience.

Apart from the traditional clubs and nightclubs, Corfu also hosts several beach parties, which are popular among visitors. These parties take place at various locations along the island's stunning coastline, including Canal d'Amour, Glyfada, and

Agios Gordios. The beach parties feature live music, DJs, and dancing, creating a fun and lively atmosphere.

Many of the clubs and nightclubs in Corfu offer a VIP experience, with bottle service, private tables, and premium seating options. These VIP services provide a more exclusive and intimate clubbing experience, allowing visitors to enjoy the party in style.

Overall, Corfu's clubbing scene offers visitors a diverse range of options, ensuring that there is something for every taste and preference. Whether you're looking for an energetic party or a more laid-back atmosphere, Corfu's clubs and nightclubs have got you covered. Just remember to drink responsibly and familiarize yourself with local customs and regulations to ensure a safe and enjoyable clubbing experience.

Live Music and Events

Corfu is a hub for live music and vibrant events that cater to a variety of musical tastes and cultural interests. Throughout the year, the island hosts an array of concerts, festivals, and performances that showcase both local talent and international artists. Whether you're a fan of classical music, traditional Greek tunes, or contemporary genres, Corfu offers a diverse range of live music experiences.

Corfu Summer Festival

The Corfu Summer Festival is a highly anticipated annual event that takes place from June to September. This festival celebrates the arts in all its forms and features a captivating lineup of concerts, theater performances, ballets, opera, and dance shows. The venues vary from open-air theaters to historic sites, providing a unique and enchanting atmosphere. It's a chance to witness exceptional performances by renowned artists and immerse yourself in the cultural richness of the island.

Traditional Greek Music

Corfu has a strong tradition of folk music and local musical styles. Various festivals and events throughout the year showcase traditional Greek music, allowing visitors to experience the authentic sounds of the island. From bouzouki melodies to lively Greek dances, you can expect a lively and joyous atmosphere during these events. Some venues, such as tavernas and local cultural centers, regularly host traditional music performances, providing an opportunity to appreciate the island's cultural heritage.

Jazz and Blues Festivals

Corfu hosts jazz and blues festivals that attract both local and international jazz enthusiasts. These events feature talented musicians, both established and emerging, who perform in scenic outdoor settings and intimate venues. The festival lineups encompass a wide range of jazz styles, including traditional jazz, Latin jazz, fusion, and smooth jazz. Blues festivals showcase soulful performances that highlight the rich history and emotional depth of the blues genre.

Beach Concerts

The stunning beaches of Corfu serve as picturesque backdrops for beach concerts and live music events during the summer months. From rock bands to electronic music DJs, these open-air concerts allow you to enjoy your favorite music while basking in the beauty of the coastline. Some popular beach bars and resorts organize regular live music events, providing a relaxed and laid-back atmosphere for music lovers.

Local Music Venues

Corfu Town and other major towns on the island offer a range of venues dedicated to live music. These establishments, including bars, clubs, and music halls, regularly host performances by local bands, solo artists, and cover bands. You can expect a vibrant and intimate atmosphere as you immerse yourself in the local music scene. Keep an eye out for announcements and flyers to discover the latest gigs and performances happening around the island.

Cultural Celebrations

Corfu's cultural celebrations often incorporate live music as an integral part of the festivities. One such event is the Easter celebrations, during which the island comes alive with processions, traditional music, and choral performances. Additionally, local religious festivals and holidays are accompanied by music and dance performances, offering visitors a chance to witness the island's cultural traditions firsthand.

Attending live music events and festivals in Corfu not only allows you to enjoy captivating performances but also provides a deeper understanding of the island's cultural heritage and artistic expression. Immerse yourself in the diverse music scene and let the melodies and rhythms of Corfu create unforgettable memories during your visit.

If you're looking for a social and adventurous night out in Corfu, participating in a pub crawl or engaging in bar hopping activities is an excellent choice. These organized events provide a fantastic opportunity to explore the island's vibrant nightlife, meet fellow travelers, and experience the local bar scene in a fun and exciting way.

Pub Crawls and Bar Hopping

Pub crawls and bar hopping activities in Corfu typically involve a group of participants led by a knowledgeable guide who takes them to various bars and pubs throughout the night. Here's what you can expect from these experiences:

Meeting Point and Group Dynamics

Pub crawls usually have a designated meeting point, often in a central location such as Corfu Town. Here, participants gather and get to know each other, creating a lively and sociable atmosphere right from the start. The groups are usually diverse, consisting of both locals and tourists of different ages and backgrounds, which adds to the dynamic and friendly nature of the experience.

Experienced Guides

The pub crawls are led by experienced guides who are well-versed in the local nightlife scene. They have extensive knowledge of the best bars, clubs, and hidden gems in Corfu, ensuring that participants have an unforgettable night out. Guides often share interesting facts about the island, provide recommendations, and ensure everyone's safety and enjoyment throughout the evening.

Bar Hopping Route

The pub crawl or bar hopping route varies depending on the organizer and the specific event. However, it typically includes visits to multiple bars and pubs, allowing participants to experience the diversity of Corfu's nightlife. The route may cover popular areas such as Corfu Town, Kavos, Ipsos, or Sidari, and can include a mix of beach bars, cocktail lounges, traditional tavernas, and lively nightclubs.

Drink Specials and Discounts

Participating in a pub crawl often comes with some perks, such as discounted drinks or exclusive deals at the venues visited. Organizers may negotiate special offers with the bars and clubs, ensuring that participants can enjoy their favorite beverages without breaking the bank. These discounts add to the affordability and value of the experience, making it even more appealing.

Live Music and Entertainment

Depending on the specific pub crawl or bar hopping event, live music and entertainment may be included. This can range from local bands and DJs performing at the venues to street performers and dancers adding to the vibrant atmosphere. The combination of great music, lively crowds, and talented performers creates a truly memorable experience for participants.

Making New Friends

One of the highlights of pub crawls and bar hopping activities is the opportunity to meet new people and make lasting connections. Sharing drinks, conversations, and laughter with fellow participants from all around the world fosters a sense of camaraderie and creates an inclusive and welcoming environment. It's a chance to swap travel stories, make friends, and forge international connections.

Safety and Responsible Drinking
While pub crawls and bar hopping can be a lot of fun, it's essential to prioritize safety and responsible drinking. Guides are trained to ensure the well-being of participants, offering guidance and support throughout the night. It's important to drink responsibly, know your limits, and always have a plan for getting back to your accommodation safely. Additionally, familiarize yourself with local laws and regulations regarding alcohol consumption.

Participating in a pub crawl or engaging in bar hopping activities in Corfu guarantees a night filled with laughter, new experiences, and memorable moments. Whether you're traveling solo, with friends, or as a couple, these social outings provide an excellent opportunity to explore the island's nightlife scene, make new friends, and create unforgettable memories.

Casino

If you're feeling lucky and enjoy a bit of gambling, Corfu offers a casino experience at the Corfu Casino located in the beautiful Kanoni area. The casino provides a range of gaming options, including slot machines, roulette, and blackjack tables, ensuring an exciting and entertaining evening for visitors looking to try their luck.

In conclusion, Corfu's nightlife is a testament to its lively and diverse character, offering visitors a chance to let loose, dance the night away, and create unforgettable memories. Remember to drink responsibly and familiarize yourself with local customs and regulations to ensure a safe and enjoyable nightlife experience.

CHAPTER EIGHT

SHOPPING IN CORFU

Corfu offers a diverse and vibrant shopping scene, where visitors can find a variety of unique items, from traditional crafts to local delicacies. Whether you're looking for souvenirs to take back home or wish to immerse yourself in the local shopping culture, Corfu has something for everyone.

Shopping Districts

Corfu offers several shopping districts where you can find a variety of shops, boutiques, and stores. Here are some notable areas for shopping in Corfu:

Liston Promenade

The Liston Promenade in Corfu Town is a picturesque area that exudes old-world charm. Lined with elegant buildings inspired by Venetian architecture, the promenade is a hub of activity and a delightful place for shopping. The shops and boutiques along the Liston Promenade offer a wide range of products, including fashionable clothing, footwear, accessories, jewelry, and local handicrafts. You'll find boutique stores showcasing designer brands as well as local artisans selling unique and handmade items. Additionally, there are shops specializing in traditional Greek products such as olive oil, herbs, spices, and local wines. As you stroll along the promenade, take in the vibrant atmosphere, stop for a coffee at one of the outdoor cafes, and explore the inviting shops that dot this iconic shopping district.

Spianada Square
Spianada Square, located adjacent to the Liston Promenade, is a bustling area in Corfu Town that offers a mix of shopping options. The square itself is a spacious and lively gathering place, often hosting cultural events and live performances. Surrounding the square, you'll find shops and boutiques catering to various tastes and interests. From trendy fashion boutiques to traditional souvenir stores, there's something for everyone. Browse through clothing stores offering the latest trends, explore accessory shops for unique jewelry and handbags, or peruse gift shops to find Corfu-themed souvenirs and keepsakes. As you shop in Spianada Square, take advantage of the vibrant energy and enjoy the blend of modern and traditional shopping experiences.

Gouvia Marina
Gouvia Marina, located near the village of Gouvia, is not only a popular mooring spot for yachts but also a delightful destination for shopping. The marina area offers a selection of shops that cater to nautical

enthusiasts and fashion lovers alike. Nautical-themed stores stock a variety of items such as boating accessories, sailing gear, and maritime-inspired decor. You can find stylish beachwear, resort wear, and accessories in boutique shops, allowing you to shop for the perfect vacation outfits. Additionally, there are stores offering local products, including olive oil, wines, herbs, and handmade crafts. Take your time to explore the marina, soak in the beautiful views of the waterfront, and indulge in some retail therapy in this charming shopping district.

Ipsos

Ipsos is a lively resort town on the northeastern coast of Corfu known for its vibrant nightlife and beautiful beach. However, it also boasts a vibrant shopping scene. The main street in Ipsos is the focal point for shopping, lined with shops and boutiques catering to tourists and locals alike. Here, you'll find a variety of stores offering beachwear, swimwear, and summer fashion. Browse through colorful sarongs, stylish hats, trendy sunglasses, and other beach essentials. The street is also home to shops selling souvenirs, such as keychains, magnets, and postcards, allowing you to take home a piece of Corfu's charm. Ipsos offers a relaxed and casual shopping experience, where you can combine your shopping excursion with leisurely strolls along the beach and breaks at local cafes or seaside tavernas.

Kassiopi

Kassiopi is a picturesque village situated on the northeast coast of Corfu, surrounded by scenic beauty and overlooking the Ionian Sea. While Kassiopi is known for its historic ruins and stunning beaches, it also offers a delightful shopping experience. The village features a mix of traditional stores and boutiques nestled along its charming streets.

Explore the local shops to find unique clothing items, including resort wear, bohemian-inspired dresses, and handmade garments. Jewelry stores showcase intricate pieces crafted from silver, gold, and semi-precious gemstones, reflecting the island's rich artistic heritage. You'll also find shops specializing in locally produced items such as olive oil, honey, herbs, and spices, allowing you to bring the flavors of Corfu home with you. Additionally, Kassiopi is home to artisans and craftsmen who create beautiful ceramics, pottery, and handmade crafts, providing an opportunity to find one-of-a-kind treasures. Take your time to explore the narrow streets, visit the boutique stores, and immerse yourself in the relaxed and authentic shopping experience that Kassiopi offers.

In each of these shopping districts, you'll find a mix of both international brands and local businesses, providing a diverse range of products and shopping experiences. Whether you're seeking fashion, jewelry, souvenirs, local specialties, or unique handmade items, Corfu's shopping districts have something to offer every visitor. Soak up the atmosphere, interact with the friendly locals, and embrace the opportunity to find hidden gems and treasures to commemorate your visit to the beautiful island of Corfu.

Markets

Corfu is home to vibrant markets where visitors can immerse themselves in the local culture, interact with friendly vendors, and find an array of enticing products. Here are some of the notable markets on the island:

Old Town Market

The Old Town Market in Corfu Town is a bustling hub of activity, located in the heart of the city. The market is a maze of narrow streets and alleys filled with stalls and shops, creating a vibrant and bustling atmosphere. One of the highlights of this market is the abundance of fresh fruits and vegetables, sourced directly from local farmers. You can find colorful displays of ripe tomatoes, juicy peaches, fragrant herbs, and a variety of other seasonal produce. The market also offers a selection of locally produced cheeses, olives, cured meats, and traditional Greek products like honey and olive oil. As you wander through the market, you'll come across stalls selling clothing, accessories, and souvenirs, including handmade crafts, pottery, and jewelry. The Old Town Market is a fantastic place to immerse yourself in the local culture, sample regional flavors, and find unique treasures to take home.

Benitses Market

Located in the picturesque coastal village of Benitses, the Benitses Market is a popular destination for both locals and visitors. This market takes place every Saturday and attracts a diverse range of vendors. One of the main highlights of the Benitses Market is the abundance of fresh seafood. You can browse through stalls offering a variety of locally caught fish, including sardines, sea bream, and octopus. Alongside the seafood, you'll find an array of colorful fruits and vegetables, locally grown and bursting with flavor. The market also features stalls selling homemade pastries, bread, herbs, spices, and other culinary delights. It's a great opportunity to taste the flavors of Corfu and witness the island's culinary traditions. In addition to the food offerings, you can explore stalls offering handmade crafts, artwork, clothing, and souvenirs, allowing you to take a piece of Corfu's charm home with you.

Acharavi Market

The Acharavi Market, nestled in the charming village of Acharavi, showcases a vibrant mix of local produce, handicrafts, and everyday essentials. As you wander through the stalls, you'll be greeted by the enticing aroma of fresh fruits and vegetables, all sourced from the surrounding fertile lands. Engage with the friendly vendors and embrace the opportunity to learn about the seasonality of Corfu's produce, gaining insights into the island's agricultural traditions.

Apart from the bountiful produce, the Acharavi Market offers an array of clothing, shoes, accessories, and household items. Browse through the stalls and you may stumble upon unique pieces crafted by local artisans, from handmade jewelry to intricately embroidered textiles.

The market is also an excellent spot to interact with the local community, as residents gather to socialize and share their stories. Embrace the warm atmosphere and immerse yourself in the island's authentic spirit.

Remember to arrive at the markets early in the morning to experience the vibrant hustle and bustle at its peak. This is when you'll find the freshest produce, have the widest selection of products, and enjoy the liveliness of the markets in full swing.

Unique Souvenirs to get

Corfu is an excellent destination for souvenir shopping. Visitors can find unique gifts and mementos that reflect the island's culture and heritage. Some popular souvenirs include:

Olive Oil

Corfu is known for its high-quality olive oil. Olive trees are abundant on the island, and the olives harvested here produce a rich and flavorful oil. Visitors can purchase bottles of local olive oil to take home or as gifts for friends and family. Look for bottles labeled "extra virgin" for the highest quality.

Handicrafts

Corfu has a rich tradition of handicrafts, and artisans on the island produce a variety of unique items. Some popular handicrafts include:

Ceramics: Corfu's pottery workshops create beautiful ceramics using traditional techniques. Visitors can find hand-painted plates, bowls, vases, and decorative items adorned with intricate patterns and vibrant colors.

Textiles: Corfu is known for its embroidery and lacework. Handmade tablecloths, linens, and clothing items featuring delicate lace patterns make for exquisite souvenirs.

Woodcarvings: Skilled woodcarvers in Corfu create intricate sculptures, decorative items, and furniture using locally sourced wood. Visitors can find unique pieces showcasing traditional Greek designs or motifs inspired by the island's natural beauty.

Traditional Greek Pottery

Corfu is home to several pottery workshops where artisans continue the age-old tradition of Greek pottery making. Visitors can find handcrafted pottery items such as amphorae, bowls, plates, and vases adorned with mythological motifs, geometric patterns, or inspired by the island's flora and fauna. These pieces serve as beautiful decorative items or functional kitchenware.

Honey

Corfu is known for its delicious honey, produced by bees that feed on the island's wildflowers. The honey has a unique flavor and aroma, making it a sought-after souvenir. Visitors can purchase jars of honey from local producers, who often offer different varieties, including thyme, pine, and wildflower honey.

Koum Kouat Liqueur

Koum Kouat is a citrus fruit native to Corfu, and the island is famous for its production of Koum Kouat liqueur. This liqueur has a distinctive taste, combining the flavors of bitter orange and spices. Visitors can find bottles of Koum Kouat liqueur, often beautifully packaged, in shops and distilleries across the island.

Kumquat Products

Aside from the liqueur, Kumquat fruit is utilized in various other products. Visitors can find Kumquat marmalades, preserves, chocolates, and candies, all featuring the unique flavor of this small citrus fruit. These products make for delicious and locally inspired gifts.

When shopping for souvenirs in Corfu, explore local markets, artisan shops, and specialty stores to find these unique items. Remember to ask the shop owners for recommendations and insights into the products, as they can provide valuable information about the craftsmanship and cultural significance of the souvenirs.

Shipping And Customs

When visiting Corfu, it's important to be aware of the customs and regulations regarding shipping and importing items into the country. Here are some important things to keep in mind:

Shipping Items Home

If you've purchased souvenirs or other items during your trip to Corfu and would like to ship them home, there are a few things to consider. Firstly, it's important to ensure that the items you are shipping are allowed to be imported into your home country.

Some items, such as certain types of food or plants, may be restricted or prohibited.

It's also important to choose a reputable shipping company that can handle your items safely and securely. Check with the company to ensure that they have experience shipping items internationally and that they have a good track record.

When packing your items for shipping, be sure to use appropriate packaging materials to ensure that they arrive at their destination in good condition. Consider using bubble wrap or packing peanuts to protect fragile items.

Customs Regulations

When entering or exiting Corfu, you'll need to go through customs. Here are some important things to keep in mind:

Declare all items: When entering or exiting the country, you'll be required to declare all items that you are carrying with you. This includes any souvenirs, gifts, or other items that you have purchased during your trip.

Restricted items: Certain items may be restricted or prohibited from entering or exiting the country. This may include certain types of food, plants, or other items that could pose a risk to the local environment or economy.

Duty fees: Depending on the items you are carrying, you may be required to pay duty fees upon entering or exiting the country. These fees can vary depending on the value and nature of the items you are carrying.

Tips for Smooth Customs Clearance

To ensure a smooth customs clearance process, it's important to be prepared. Here are some tips:

Keep your documents organized: Make sure you have all of the necessary documents, such as your passport and any relevant visas, organized and easily accessible.

Declare all items: Be sure to declare all items that you are carrying, even if they are small or of low value.

Follow customs regulations: Make sure you are aware of the customs regulations for both Corfu and your home country, and follow them closely.

Be patient: Customs clearance can be a slow process, so be patient and allow plenty of time for the process.

By following these tips and being aware of the customs regulations for shipping and importing items into Corfu, you can ensure a smooth and hassle-free experience when traveling.

Shopping Tips And Recommendation

Engage with the locals: The vendors in Corfu's markets are often passionate about their products and eager to share their knowledge. Strike up conversations, ask questions, and listen to their stories. Not only will you gain insights into the local culture, but you may also discover hidden gems and receive recommendations for the best products.

Taste the flavors: Many vendors offer samples of their products, especially when it comes to food items like olives, cheeses, and honey. Don't hesitate to try before you buy. Sampling allows you to fully appreciate the unique flavors of Corfu and make informed decisions about your purchases.

Embrace the haggling culture: Haggling is a common practice in Corfu's markets, and it adds an element of excitement to the shopping experience. Engage in friendly negotiations with the vendors, keeping in mind that the goal is to find a mutually agreeable price. Remember to be respectful and enjoy the process of bargaining, which is deeply ingrained in the local culture.

Don't be afraid to negotiate the price, especially for souvenirs and handicrafts. Polite haggling can often lead to discounts or better deals.

Opening Hours: Most shops in Corfu are open from Monday to Saturday, with a break during the afternoon (siesta) when many businesses close for a few hours. Larger stores and supermarkets usually stay open throughout the day. On Sundays, the majority of shops are closed, except for some tourist-oriented areas.

Authentic Handicrafts: Corfu has a rich tradition of handicrafts, including ceramics, textiles, and woodwork. To ensure you're purchasing authentic local crafts, look for shops that specialize in handmade products or visit local artisan workshops where you can observe the craftsmen at work.

Shipping: If you've made larger purchases or bought fragile items, inquire about shipping options. Many shops can arrange to have your purchases shipped to your home address, ensuring their safe delivery.

Popular Shopping Areas: Corfu Town is the main shopping hub on the island, with a variety of shops and boutiques. The Liston and Spianada areas are particularly popular for luxury brands and designer stores. For a more traditional shopping experience, explore the narrow streets of the Old Town, where you'll find shops selling a wide range of items, from clothing to local products.

Explore beyond the market stalls: While the markets themselves are vibrant and captivating, don't hesitate to venture into the surrounding streets. Corfu's towns and villages are often filled with shops, boutiques, and local artisans offering unique products. Take the time to explore these hidden gems and discover additional treasures that may not be found within the market confines.

Bring cash: While some vendors may accept credit cards, it's advisable to carry cash, especially for smaller purchases. ATMs are readily available in most towns and villages, ensuring you have easy access to the local currency.

Plan for transportation: If you're visiting markets located outside the main towns, such as Benitses or Acharavi, consider arranging transportation in advance. Public transportation options may be limited, so a taxi or rental car can provide flexibility and convenience.

Overall, if you're looking for unique souvenirs or fresh local produce, Corfu offers a wide range of shopping options to suit every taste and budget.

In conclusion, exploring these markets provides a wonderful opportunity to engage with the local community, experience the island's vibrant atmosphere, and discover unique treasures. Visitors can sample delicious Greek treats, such as freshly baked pastries and traditional sweets, as they meander through the colorful stalls. Bargaining is often welcome, so feel free to negotiate prices and strike a good deal. The markets of Corfu offer an authentic and memorable shopping experience, where visitors can connect with the island's rich traditions and take home a piece of its vibrant culture.

CHAPTER NINE

EVENTS AND FESTIVALS

Corfu is a vibrant island that embraces its rich cultural heritage through a variety of lively events and colorful festivals. Whether you're seeking traditional customs, music and dance performances, or culinary delights, Corfu's calendar is filled with exciting celebrations that offer visitors a unique and immersive experience. From religious processions to summer festivals and wine celebrations, there's always something happening on the island. Join the locals in their joyous festivities and discover the spirit of Corfu through its events and festivals.

Easter Celebrations

Corfu is renowned for its vibrant Easter celebrations, which attract visitors from all over the world. The festivities combine religious traditions with a unique local flair. On Holy Saturday, locals and visitors gather in Corfu Town to witness the "Botides," a custom where large clay pots are thrown from balconies, smashing into the streets below. This act symbolizes the earthquake that occurred when Jesus was crucified. The spectacle is accompanied by music, fireworks, and a lively atmosphere. On Easter Sunday, the town is filled with processions, including the procession of the Epitaph, where the locals march through the streets carrying a decorated bier. The atmosphere is electric, and the celebrations continue throughout the day with feasting and traditional music and dance.

Corfu Summer Festival

The Corfu Summer Festival is an annual cultural extravaganza that takes place from June to September, enchanting both locals and visitors alike. With a lineup that showcases a diverse range of artistic disciplines, the festival has become one of the highlights of Corfu's cultural calendar. From theater performances to musical concerts, ballet and dance shows to art exhibitions, the Corfu Summer Festival offers a captivating array of events that cater to different artistic tastes.

One of the festival's iconic venues is the historic Old Fortress, located in Corfu Town. This imposing fortress, with its stunning backdrop of the Ionian Sea, provides a majestic setting for theatrical performances and concerts. The open-air theater within the fortress walls offers a unique atmosphere, where audiences can immerse themselves in the magic of live performances while enjoying the cool sea breeze.

The Liston promenade, located in the heart of Corfu Town, is another vibrant venue that hosts various festival events. Lined with elegant cafés and arcades, the Liston exudes a sophisticated ambiance that perfectly complements the artistic flair of the festival. Here, visitors can witness captivating dance performances, musical recitals, and even street theater, all against the backdrop of the town's architectural splendor.

The festival program features both local and international artists, providing a platform for cultural exchange and artistic collaboration. Acclaimed theater troupes, renowned orchestras, and world-class soloists grace the stages of the Corfu Summer Festival, offering unforgettable performances that showcase the highest levels of artistic excellence.

In addition to theater and music, the festival also celebrates visual arts with curated exhibitions. Local and international artists display their works in galleries and exhibition spaces throughout Corfu Town, allowing visitors to immerse themselves in the rich and diverse world of visual creativity.

The Corfu Summer Festival is not limited to established artists; it also supports emerging talents through dedicated platforms and showcases. Young performers and artists are given opportunities to shine, fostering a dynamic and innovative arts scene on the island.

Beyond the performances, the festival creates a vibrant atmosphere throughout Corfu Town. The streets come alive with cultural events, street performances, and impromptu concerts, providing a lively backdrop for visitors to immerse themselves in the island's artistic spirit. The festival also often collaborates with local businesses, such as restaurants and bars, to offer special promotions and themed events that further enhance the overall festival experience.

Attending the Corfu Summer Festival offers a unique opportunity to engage with the island's cultural heritage, witness outstanding artistic performances, and create lasting memories. The festival's diverse and engaging program ensures that there is something for everyone, from classical music enthusiasts to theater aficionados and art lovers. Immerse yourself in the creative energy of Corfu and let the Corfu Summer Festival captivate your senses with its captivating performances and cultural offerings.

Wine Festivals

Corfu has a long tradition of wine production, and during the harvest season, several wine festivals are held across the island. These festivals celebrate the island's viticulture and offer an opportunity to sample a variety of local wines. The festivals typically include wine tastings, traditional music and dance performances, and delicious local cuisine. Visitors can learn about the winemaking process, interact with local producers, and immerse themselves in the island's wine culture. The wine festivals provide a festive and convivial atmosphere, making them a delightful experience for wine enthusiasts and cultural enthusiasts alike.

Carnival

One of the most anticipated and exuberant events on the island is the Carnival of Corfu, a grand celebration of music, dance, and colorful costumes. The Carnival season kicks off in January and culminates in a week-long extravaganza leading up to Clean Monday, which marks the beginning of Lent.

The Carnival festivities are deeply rooted in Corfu's history and traditions, dating back centuries. Influenced by Venetian and French customs, the Carnival of Corfu blends elements of satire, humor, and revelry. Locals and visitors alike participate in the merriment, creating a vibrant and jovial atmosphere throughout the island.

The centerpiece of the Carnival is the grand parade that takes place in Corfu Town. Elaborately decorated floats, adorned with intricate designs and themes, parade through the streets accompanied by enthusiastic revelers. Participants dress in elaborate costumes, ranging from traditional folk attire to imaginative and humorous outfits. The parade is a visual spectacle, with vibrant colors, lively music, and dancing filling the air.

One of the distinctive features of the Carnival of Corfu is the "Kaparelli" or "Kantades." During the evenings leading up to the main parade, groups of people gather in the streets and sing satirical songs, often targeting social and political figures. This tradition harks back to the Venetian era when masked performers would roam the streets, entertaining and mocking the ruling class.

The festivities continue late into the night, with parties, street performances, and live music filling the squares and tavernas. The joyful ambiance is contagious as locals and visitors come together to celebrate the spirit of Carnival.

Children also play a significant role in the Carnival celebrations, with schools organizing their own parades and costume competitions. Families gather to enjoy the festivities, and children delight in dressing up as their favorite characters and joining the procession.

The Carnival of Corfu is a time of uninhibited revelry and a break from the norms of everyday life. It is a celebration of community, creativity, and the island's cultural heritage. Visitors have the opportunity to immerse themselves in the vibrant energy, witness the unique traditions, and experience the joyous spirit that permeates the island during this time.

If you plan to visit Corfu during Carnival, be sure to check the official schedule, as the dates may vary each year. Embrace the festive atmosphere, join in the parades, and don't forget to dress up and unleash your own inner reveler during this exciting time on the island of Corfu.

Music Festivals

Corfu also hosts various music festivals throughout the year, catering to different genres and tastes. From classical music concerts in historic venues to contemporary music festivals on the beach, there is something for everyone. The festivals often feature renowned local and international artists, showcasing a diverse range of musical styles. Whether you're a fan of classical, jazz, rock, or traditional Greek music, you're likely to find a festival that caters to your musical preferences during your visit to Corfu.

International Documentary Festival

The International Documentary Festival of Corfu is an annual event that celebrates the art of documentary filmmaking. Held in Corfu Town, the festival showcases a selection of thought-provoking and engaging documentaries from around the world. It provides a platform for filmmakers to present their work and encourages discussions on important social, cultural, and environmental issues. The festival attracts film enthusiasts, industry professionals, and documentary filmmakers, creating a vibrant atmosphere of cinematic exploration and discovery.

Corfu Beer Festival

For beer lovers, the Corfu Beer Festival is a must-visit event. Held in Arillas, a charming coastal village, this festival celebrates the craft beer industry and offers a variety of local and international brews to sample. The festival features live music, food stalls serving delicious snacks, and a relaxed and friendly ambiance. It's a great opportunity to taste unique beers, socialize with fellow beer enthusiasts, and enjoy the laid-back atmosphere of a beachside festival.

Religious Festivals

Corfu has a strong religious heritage, and throughout the year, various religious festivals take place on the island. These festivals are deeply rooted in the local culture and traditions. One such festival is the Feast of St. Spyridon, the patron saint of Corfu. Celebrated on December 12th, the day is marked by religious processions, church services, and festive gatherings. Another notable religious event is the Feast of Virgin Mary on August 15th, where processions and religious services take place in churches across the island.

Olive Oil Festivals

As an island known for its olive groves and high-quality olive oil, Corfu hosts several olive oil festivals. These festivals highlight the importance of olive oil in the local cuisine and culture. Visitors can witness olive oil production demonstrations, participate in olive oil tastings, and learn about the traditional methods of olive oil extraction. These festivals also offer an opportunity to purchase authentic Corfiot olive oil directly from local producers.

Traditional Music and Dance Festivals

Throughout the year, Corfu showcases its rich musical heritage through traditional music and dance festivals. These events bring together local musicians and dancers to perform traditional Greek folk music and dances. The festivals offer a glimpse into the island's cultural heritage and provide an immersive experience for visitors to enjoy the lively rhythms and captivating movements of traditional Greek music and dance.

Please keep in mind that the specific dates and details of events and festivals may vary from year to year. It is advisable to check the latest information and schedules closer to your travel dates to ensure you don't miss out on any events during your visit to Corfu.

In conclusion, Corfu's events and festivals offer an exciting glimpse into the island's cultural heritage and provide visitors with a chance to immerse themselves in the local traditions. Whether you choose to witness the grandeur of the Easter celebrations, embrace the artistic flair of the Corfu Summer Festival, or indulge in the wine festivities, these events showcase the island's vibrant spirit and its people's deep-rooted connection to their heritage. Plan your visit to coincide with these celebrations, and you'll be rewarded with a truly memorable and authentic experience in Corfu.

CHAPTER TEN

MY 19 TO DO LIST FOR AN UNFORGETTABLE EXPERIENCE IN CORFU

Corfu, with its stunning beaches, rich history, and vibrant culture, offers a multitude of experiences that can create unforgettable memories for every traveler. Whether you're seeking adventure, relaxation, or cultural immersion, this diverse Greek island has something to offer. To make the most of your time in Corfu, here is a comprehensive list of 19 must-do activities and experiences that will ensure an unforgettable stay.

1. **Explore the charming streets of Corfu Town, a UNESCO World Heritage site, and immerse yourself in its Venetian-style architecture, narrow alleys, and vibrant atmosphere.**

   - Stroll along the Liston, a promenade lined with cafes, where you can sip on a refreshing drink and people-watch.

- Visit the Old Venetian Fortress and climb to the top for panoramic views of the town and the sea.

- Explore the Old Town's labyrinthine streets, discovering hidden gems, such as quaint shops, local markets, and traditional tavernas.

2. **Relax on the beautiful beaches of Glyfada, Sidari, or Paleokastritsa and soak up the sun while enjoying the crystal-clear waters of the Ionian Sea.**

- Spend a day lounging on the soft sandy beaches, swimming in the turquoise waters, and basking in the Mediterranean sunshine.

- Engage in water sports activities, including jet skiing, parasailing, or paddleboarding, for an adrenaline-filled experience.

- Take a leisurely boat tour along the coastline, exploring hidden coves, caves, and secluded beaches.

3. **Visit the iconic Old Fortress in Corfu Town, climb its ancient walls, and admire panoramic views of the city and the sea.**

   - Explore the fortress's historical exhibits and learn about its strategic importance throughout the centuries.

   - Capture stunning photos of Corfu Town and the surrounding landscape from the fortress's vantage points.

   - Attend special events or concerts held within the fortress during the summer months for a unique cultural experience.

4. **Take a boat tour to the enchanting sea caves of Paleokastritsa and marvel at the stunning natural formations and the vibrant colors of the water.**

   - Board a boat and navigate through the crystal-clear waters, exploring the intricate network of caves.

   - Witness the awe-inspiring stalactites and stalagmites, which have been shaped by the sea's erosive forces over thousands of years.

- Dive into the refreshing waters and snorkel to discover the diverse marine life that thrives in and around the caves.

5. **Discover the Achilleion Palace, a grand neoclassical mansion built for Empress Elisabeth of Austria, and explore its beautiful gardens and stunning views.**

- Admire the opulent interior adorned with statues, paintings, and ornate decorations that reflect the palace's regal history.

- Wander through the palace's manicured gardens, which feature statues inspired by Greek mythology and offer breathtaking vistas of the surrounding landscape.

- Learn about the life of Empress Elisabeth and her connection to Corfu through informative displays and exhibits.

6. **Go on a hike along the Corfu Trail, a 220-kilometer long-distance footpath that traverses the island, offering**

breathtaking vistas of the coastline and countryside.

- Choose a section of the trail that suits your fitness level and embark on a scenic hike, immersing yourself in Corfu's natural beauty.

- Encounter picturesque villages, olive groves, vineyards, and charming rural landscapes as you follow the trail.

- Take breaks at scenic viewpoints to appreciate the panoramic views of the Ionian Sea and the lush greenery of the island.

7. **Indulge in a traditional Greek feast at a local taverna, savoring dishes like moussaka, souvlaki, and fresh seafood paired with a glass of local wine.**

- Explore the quaint streets of Corfu Town or coastal villages to find traditional tavernas known for their authentic cuisine.

- Sample a variety of mezes (appetizers) like tzatziki, dolmades, and feta cheese, accompanied by warm bread.

- Enjoy a leisurely meal, soaking up the relaxed ambiance and the warm hospitality of the locals. Don't forget to try local specialties like bourdeto (spicy fish stew) and pastitsada (slow-cooked meat with pasta), which are unique to Corfu.

8. **Attend a traditional Greek music and dance performance, where you can witness the lively rhythms and graceful movements that are deeply ingrained in Corfu's cultural heritage**.

   - Look out for local festivals or cultural events where traditional music and dance performances take place.

   - Enjoy the melodic tunes of the bouzouki, violin, and accordion, accompanied by energetic dances like syrtos and kalamatianos.

   - Consider taking part in a Greek dance workshop, where you can learn the steps and join in the fun with locals and fellow travelers.

9. **Visit the Museum of Asian Art in Corfu Town and explore its impressive collection of artworks from various Asian countries, showcasing the island's historical connections with the East.**

- Marvel at the intricately crafted statues, ceramics, and textiles from China, Japan, India, and other Asian countries.

- Gain insight into the historical trade routes and cultural exchanges between Corfu and the East.

- Take your time to appreciate the delicate details and symbolism portrayed in the exhibited artworks.

10. **Embark on a day trip to the nearby island of Paxos, known for its turquoise waters, charming villages, and tranquil atmosphere.**

- Hop on a ferry from Corfu Town and enjoy a scenic boat ride to the picturesque island of Paxos.

- Explore the idyllic coastal villages of Gaios, Lakka, and Loggos, with their colorful houses and charming harbors.

- Discover hidden beaches and secluded coves, where you can swim, snorkel, or simply unwind in a peaceful setting.

11. **Explore the traditional villages of Pelekas, Benitses, and Agios Mattheos, immersing yourself in the local culture, architecture, and authentic way of life.**

- Wander through the narrow streets, observing the traditional stone houses and charming squares.

- Visit local workshops and artisans to witness traditional crafts, such as pottery, weaving, and olive wood carving.

- Engage with the friendly locals, learn about their customs, and savor the slow-paced lifestyle of these quaint villages.

12. **Take a scenic drive to Mount Pantokrator, the highest peak on the island, and enjoy panoramic views of Corfu and the surrounding islands from its summit.**

- Drive or join a guided tour to Mount Pantokrator, which offers stunning vistas along the way.

- Reach the summit and admire the breathtaking views of the Ionian Sea, Albania, and neighboring islands.

- Visit the 17th-century monastery located near the peak and explore its beautiful gardens and religious artifacts.

13. **Visit the Mon Repos Palace, a neoclassical gem surrounded by lush gardens, and discover its fascinating history and connections to the Greek royal family.**

- Explore the palace's elegant rooms and learn about its transformation from a villa to a summer residence for the Greek royal family.

- Stroll through the peaceful gardens, filled with Mediterranean flora and fauna, and enjoy the serene ambiance.

- Learn about the birth of Prince Philip, Duke of Edinburgh, who was born at Mon Repos, and the palace's significance in the royal family's history.

14. **Engage in water sports activities such as snorkeling, kayaking, or paddleboarding, and explore the hidden coves and underwater treasures along the coast.**

- Rent equipment from beachside vendors or join organized tours to explore the marine wonders of Corfu.

- Snorkel in clear waters to observe colorful fish, vibrant corals, and other marine life.

- Paddle along the coastline, discovering secluded beaches, sea caves, and impressive rock formations that are only accessible by water.

15. **Attend the Carnival of Corfu, a lively and colorful celebration filled with parades, costumes, music, and dancing, showcasing the island's vibrant spirit and cultural traditions.**

- Join the locals and visitors in the streets of Corfu Town during the Carnival season, typically in February or March.

- Witness the extravagant floats, adorned with elaborate decorations and imaginative themes, as they parade through the town.

- Dress up in a costume or mask and join the festivities, dancing to the lively rhythms of traditional music and soaking in the joyful atmosphere.

16. **Wander through the Olive Grove Trail, a scenic path that winds through ancient olive groves, providing a tranquil escape and a chance to connect with nature.**

- Follow the well-marked trail and meander through the peaceful countryside, surrounded by centuries-old olive trees.

- Breathe in the fresh air and enjoy the soothing ambiance of the groves, while learning about the olive oil production process and the importance of olives in Corfu's economy.

- Stop at viewpoints along the trail to take in panoramic views of the landscape and capture memorable photographs.

17.   **Experience the unique gastronomy of Corfu by participating in a cooking class where you can learn to prepare traditional dishes using local ingredients and flavors.**

- Enroll in a cooking workshop led by local chefs, who will guide you through the preparation of classic Corfiot dishes.

- Learn about the island's culinary traditions, including the use of fresh herbs, local produce, and traditional cooking techniques.

- Enjoy the fruits of your labor as you indulge in a delicious meal, savoring the authentic flavors of Corfu.

18.   **Discover the underwater world of Corfu through a scuba diving excursion, exploring the vibrant marine life, hidden caves, and intriguing shipwrecks beneath the sea.**

- Join a certified diving center that offers guided dives suitable for all experience levels.

- Dive into the clear waters of the Ionian Sea, encountering colorful fish, fascinating rock formations, and diverse marine ecosystems.

- Explore underwater caves and swim alongside shipwrecks, such as the HMHS Britannic or the USS Saros, which have become habitats for marine species.

19. **Witness the stunning sunset views from the charming village of Pelekas, perched atop a hill, offering breathtaking panoramas of the island's coastline.**

- Make your way to the village of Pelekas in the late afternoon to capture the mesmerizing sunset.

- Climb up to the Kaiser's Throne viewpoint, where you can enjoy unobstructed vistas of the sea, mountains, and the sun setting on the horizon.

- Relax and soak in the magical atmosphere as the sky transforms into hues of orange, pink, and purple, creating a picture-perfect moment to end your day in Corfu.

By immersing yourself in these diverse experiences, you will create cherished memories and a deep connection to the beauty and culture of Corfu, ensuring an unforgettable and fulfilling journey on this enchanting Greek island.

CHAPTER ELEVEN

PRACTICAL INFORMATION

Corfu is a unique and diverse travel destination with a rich culture and stunning natural beauty. As with any travel destination, it is important to have some practical information on hand before embarking on your trip.

Before embarking on your journey to Corfu, it's helpful to familiarize yourself with some practical information to ensure a smooth and enjoyable trip. Here are some of the essential information you should familiarize yourself with on your trip to Corfu

Transportation

Corfu offers various transportation options to help you navigate the island effectively.

Buses

Corfu has an extensive bus network that connects major towns and popular tourist destinations. The main bus terminal is located in Corfu Town, and you can find schedules and ticket information at the terminal or online. Buses are a cost-effective way to explore the island, and the routes cover most areas of interest.

Taxis

Taxis are readily available throughout Corfu, particularly in tourist areas and near the airport and port. They provide a convenient and flexible mode of transportation, allowing you to reach your destination quickly. Make sure the taxi has a working meter or negotiate the fare before starting your journey.

Car Rentals

Renting a car is a popular option for exploring Corfu, offering flexibility and the freedom to visit remote areas at your own pace. Several car rental agencies operate on the island, both at the airport and in major towns. Ensure you have an international driving permit if required and familiarize yourself with local traffic regulations.

Weather and Best Time to Visit

Corfu enjoys a Mediterranean climate, characterized by mild winters and hot summers. Here's an overview of the seasons:

Spring (March to May)

Spring in Corfu brings pleasant temperatures, with an average high of 20°C (68°F) in April. The island blooms with colorful flowers, making it an ideal time for nature walks and exploring the countryside. The sea might still be a bit cool for swimming but is generally suitable for water sports.

Summer (June to August)

Summer is the peak tourist season in Corfu, with temperatures ranging from 25°C to 35°C (77°F to 95°F). The island is bustling with visitors, and all tourist facilities, including beaches, restaurants, and attractions, are in full swing. The sea is warm and perfect for swimming and water activities.

Autumn (September to November)

Autumn in Corfu offers pleasant temperatures, with an average high of around 25°C (77°F) in September. The island becomes less crowded, and the sea remains warm enough for swimming. It's a great time to explore Corfu's cultural attractions and enjoy outdoor activities without the peak-season crowds.

Winter (December to February)

Winter in Corfu is mild, with temperatures ranging from 10°C to 15°C (50°F to 59°F). While many tourist facilities operate at a reduced capacity, the island retains its charm, and you can experience a quieter side of Corfu. Some attractions may have limited opening hours during this period.

Currency and Banking

The official currency in Corfu, as in the rest of Greece, is the Euro (€). ATMs are widely available in major towns and tourist areas, allowing you to withdraw cash. Credit cards are generally accepted in hotels, restaurants, and larger establishments, but it's a good idea to carry some cash for smaller establishments and markets.

Language

The official language of Corfu is Greek, and most locals speak Greek. However, due to the island's popularity among tourists, English is widely spoken in tourist areas, hotels, and restaurants. You will have no trouble communicating in English, but learning a few basic Greek phrases can enhance your experience.

Health and Safety

Corfu is generally a safe destination for travelers, but it's always important to prioritize your health and safety. Here are some additional tips to ensure a safe and healthy trip:

Medical Facilities

Corfu has well-equipped medical facilities, including hospitals, clinics, and pharmacies, especially in larger towns and tourist areas. If you require medical assistance, seek help from the nearest medical facility. It is recommended to have travel insurance that covers medical emergencies and hospitalization.

Travel Vaccinations

Before traveling to Corfu, it's advisable to consult your healthcare provider or a travel medicine specialist to ensure you are up to date with routine vaccinations. They may also recommend additional vaccinations based on your specific travel plans and medical history.

Sun Safety

Corfu enjoys a sunny climate, especially during the summer months. Protect yourself from the strong Mediterranean sun by following these guidelines:

- Apply sunscreen with a high SPF (sun protection factor) on all exposed skin, including face, arms, and legs.

- Wear a wide-brimmed hat, sunglasses, and lightweight, loose-fitting clothing to protect yourself from direct sun exposure.

- Seek shade during the hottest hours of the day, typically between 11 am and 3 pm.

- Stay hydrated by drinking plenty of water, especially when spending time outdoors.

Food and Water Safety

While the tap water in Corfu is generally safe to drink, some people may have more sensitive stomachs. If you prefer, you can purchase bottled water, which is widely available in supermarkets and stores across the island.

When it comes to food safety:

- Ensure that meat, seafood, and dairy products are thoroughly cooked before consuming.

- Wash fruits and vegetables with clean water or peel them before eating.

- Choose restaurants and food establishments with good hygiene practices and high customer turnover.

- Avoid eating street food from vendors whose food hygiene practices are questionable.

Insect Precautions

Corfu, like many other destinations, has its share of insects, particularly mosquitoes. To protect yourself from insect bites and reduce the risk of insect-borne diseases, consider the following:

- Use insect repellent containing DEET on exposed skin and clothing.

- Wear long-sleeved shirts, long pants, and socks in areas where mosquitoes are prevalent, especially during dusk and dawn when they are most active.

- Use mosquito nets or screens provided in accommodations or consider using a portable mosquito net for added protection while sleeping.

Emergency Contacts

Knowing the emergency contact numbers in Corfu is crucial to ensure your safety and well-being during your visit. Here are the emergency numbers you should be aware of:

General Emergency - 112

The emergency number 112 can be dialed from any phone, including mobile phones, to reach the general emergency services in Corfu. This number is a unified emergency hotline that connects you to police, ambulance services, and fire departments.

Police - 100

In case of any criminal activity, accidents, or other situations that require police assistance, dial 100 to contact the police. The police in Corfu are responsible for maintaining public order and safety.

Ambulance Service - 166

If you or someone around you requires urgent medical attention or medical transport, dial 166 to contact the ambulance service in Corfu. Trained medical professionals will respond to the emergency and provide the necessary medical assistance.

Tourist Police - +30 26610 39503

The Tourist Police in Corfu specifically cater to the needs and concerns of tourists. They can provide assistance, guidance, and information related to tourist activities, safety, and any other issues you may encounter during your visit. The phone number provided is for the Tourist Police station in Corfu, and they are usually proficient in English and other languages commonly spoken by tourists.

When making an emergency call, it's important to remain calm and provide clear and concise information about the situation, your location, and any specific details that can aid the emergency responders. If possible, try to have a local or someone fluent in Greek assist you during the call.

Note that these emergency numbers are for immediate assistance during critical situations. For non-emergency situations or general inquiries, you can contact the local police station, medical facilities, or your accommodation for guidance and assistance.

Being aware of the emergency contact numbers and knowing how to access help in Corfu will provide you with peace of mind and ensure that you receive prompt assistance in case of any emergency or crisis situation.

Communication and Internet Access

Corfu offers good communication and internet access facilities:

Mobile Network: Greek mobile network providers offer coverage throughout the island. Ensure your mobile phone is unlocked for international use or consider purchasing a local SIM card for better rates.

Wi-Fi: Most hotels, restaurants, and cafes in tourist areas provide free Wi-Fi access. Additionally, there are internet cafes available in major towns if you need a reliable internet connection.

Electric Power

The standard voltage in Corfu is 230V, and the frequency is 50Hz. The power outlets are of Type C and F, with two round-pin plugs. If your devices use a different plug type, you may need a travel adapter.

Time Zone

Corfu operates on Eastern European Time (EET), which is UTC+2. During daylight saving time, it follows Eastern European Summer Time (EEST), which is UTC+3. Make sure to adjust your clocks accordingly.

Tourist Information Centers

Corfu has several tourist information centers that can provide maps, brochures, and assistance with travel arrangements. The main tourist information center is located in Corfu Town, but you can also find smaller information points in popular tourist areas.

Customs and Duty-Free

When entering Corfu, you must adhere to the customs regulations:

Duty-Free Allowances: EU regulations apply for duty-free allowances, allowing you to bring in certain quantities of goods, including alcohol and tobacco, without incurring customs duties.

Prohibited Items: There are restrictions on bringing in certain items such as drugs, weapons, and counterfeit goods. Familiarize yourself with the customs regulations to avoid any legal issues.

Travel Insurance

It's highly recommended to have travel insurance that covers medical emergencies, trip cancellations, and lost or stolen belongings. Check with your insurance provider to ensure you have adequate coverage for your trip to Corfu.

Useful Websites And Resources For Your Corfu Trip

When planning your trip to Corfu, there are several useful websites and resources you can use to help you make the most of your time on the island. Here are some of the top ones:

Visit Greece

The official tourism website of Greece offers comprehensive information about Corfu, including highlights, attractions, accommodations, and practical advice.

Discover Corfu

This website provides in-depth insights into Corfu's history, culture, beaches, and attractions. It also offers travel tips, suggested itineraries, and recommendations for things to do.

TripAdvisor

A popular travel platform, TripAdvisor offers reviews and recommendations from fellow travelers. You can find information about hotels, restaurants, attractions, and activities in Corfu, along with user ratings and feedback.

Corfu Airport

The official website of Corfu International Airport provides up-to-date flight information, services available at the airport, transportation options to and from the airport, and other essential details for air travelers.

Corfu Port Authority

If you're arriving by ferry or planning to explore neighboring islands, the Corfu Port Authority website offers information on ferry schedules, ticket prices, and port facilities.

Corfu Public Transportation

This website provides details on bus schedules, routes, and fares for getting around Corfu by public transport. It's a useful resource for planning your itinerary and navigating the island.

Weather.com

Stay updated on the weather conditions in Corfu by accessing the website of The Weather Channel. Check the forecast, temperature, and precipitation to plan your activities accordingly.

Corfu Beach Guide

A comprehensive guide to the beaches of Corfu, offering details on their locations, facilities, water sports activities, and nearby attractions. It helps you choose the perfect beach for your preferences.

Corfu Events Calendar

Check local event listings and festivals happening during your visit to Corfu. Websites like www.corfuevents.gr or local tourism websites often provide updated event calendars, allowing you to immerse yourself in the island's culture and celebrations.

Google Translate

Google Translate can be especially useful for communicating with locals who may not speak English. Google Translate is a free translation app that allows you to translate text and speech in real-time. It's a great resource for communicating with locals and navigating the island. You can also use the app to take photos of signs or menus and receive instant translations. Download the Greek language pack to access translations offline and communicate with locals more easily.

However, keep in mind that machine translations like Google Translate are not always perfect, and there may be nuances in language or culture that the app may not fully capture.

Booking.com

A popular platform that offers a vast selection of hotels, resorts, apartments, and villas in Corfu. It provides detailed information, user reviews, and competitive rates.

Corfu City Pass

An online platform that offers discounted tickets and passes for various attractions, tours, and activities in Corfu. It helps you save money and conveniently book experiences in advance.

Offline Maps and Travel Apps

Before your trip, download offline maps or travel apps like Google Maps, MAPS.ME, or TripIt to navigate Corfu without relying on constant internet access. These apps often provide recommendations for nearby attractions, restaurants, and accommodations as well.

Overall, these websites and resources will provide you with valuable information and assistance for planning your trip to Corfu, you can gather information, plan your itinerary, and make informed decisions to ensure a memorable and enjoyable trip to Corfu.

In conclusion, by considering these practical aspects, you can make the most of your visit to Corfu and ensure a memorable and hassle-free experience on this enchanting Greek island. Enjoy the natural beauty, immerse yourself in the rich culture, and create lasting memories during your time in Corfu.

CONCLUSION

Corfu is a captivating destination that offers a perfect blend of natural beauty, rich history, and vibrant culture. Whether you're seeking relaxation on its stunning beaches, exploring its historical sites, indulging in delicious cuisine, or immersing yourself in its lively nightlife, Corfu has something for everyone.

With its convenient air and sea connections, getting to Corfu is relatively easy. The island provides a wide range of accommodation options, from luxurious resorts to cozy villas and apartments, ensuring a comfortable stay for all travelers.

Corfu's attractions are diverse and plentiful. From its breathtaking beaches and picturesque villages to its ancient fortresses and fascinating museums, there is no shortage of things to see and do. The island's natural beauty, including its lush landscapes and scenic hiking trails, offers a perfect escape for nature enthusiasts.

Food lovers will delight in Corfu's unique culinary offerings, combining Greek, Italian, and British influences. Exploring the local cuisine and indulging in the island's renowned wines is a must-do experience.

In the evenings, Corfu comes alive with its vibrant nightlife. From bustling bars and clubs to charming tavernas, there are plenty of options for entertainment and socializing.

Lastly, don't forget to explore the local markets for souvenirs and authentic products that capture the essence of Corfu. From handicrafts to local delicacies, you'll find plenty of treasures to take back home.

Corfu truly has it all—natural beauty, historical landmarks, cultural richness, culinary delights, and a lively atmosphere. Whether you're a beach lover, history enthusiast, or simply seeking an unforgettable vacation experience, Corfu is a destination that will leave a lasting impression.

As you plan your trip to Corfu, keep in mind that this guide is just the beginning. Corfu is a dynamic and ever-changing Island in Greek, with new attractions and experiences popping up all the time. So don't be afraid to explore beyond the pages of this guidebook and discover the Island for yourself.

We hope this guide has provided you with the inspiration and information you need to plan an unforgettable trip to Corfu. It doesn't matter if you're visiting for the first time or returning for a repeat visit, we know you will fall in love with this beautiful city and all that it has to offer.

ON A FINAL NOTE

The information provided in this travel guide is intended for general informational purposes as diligent effort has been made to ensure the accuracy of the information provided. Readers are solely responsible for their own travel decisions and activities and should use their judgment when following the suggestions and recommendations provided in this guide. Note that prices, hours of operation, and other details are subject to change without notice. It is always advisable to check with the relevant authorities, businesses, or organizations before making any travel plans or reservations.

The inclusion of any specific product, service, business, or organization in this guide does not constitute an endorsement by the author. Readers are advised to take necessary precautions and follow local laws, regulations, and customs. The author and publisher of this travel guide are not responsible for any inaccuracies or omissions, nor for any damages or losses that may result from following the information provided in this guide.

Thank you for choosing this CORFU TRAVEL GUIDE, and bon voyage!

MY TRAVEL NOTES

....

....

....

....

....

....

....

....

....

....

....

....

....

....

....

....

Printed in Great Britain
by Amazon

46379625R00145